THE
EVERYTHING
VEGETARIAN SLOW COOKER COOKBOOK

For many busy families, like ours, slow cookers are essential tools that help you save time in the kitchen so you can spend more with your loved ones. At the start of a busy work day, you can toss your ingredients into the pot, cover it, and go. When you walk in the door from work or after your child's soccer practice, dinner is served! But this no-fuss method doesn't mean you have to sacrifice flavor or nutrition. *The Everything® Vegetarian Slow Cooker Cookbook* features 300 full-flavored recipes from around the globe.

Whether you're a vegan, vegetarian, or a meat eater, this book is for you. Every recipe can be made vegan or vegetarian, and vegan substitutions are listed in the ingredients lists. If you're not vegan but want to eat healthier meals that are lower in fat and contain zero cholesterol, why not try a few of the vegan versions? These recipes won't leave you missing the meat, dairy, or eggs!

From our kitchen to yours, we hope you enjoy.

Amy Snyder

Justin Snyder

Welcome to the EVERYTHING® Series!

These handy, accessible books give you all you need to tackle a difficult project, gain a new hobby, comprehend a fascinating topic, prepare for an exam, or even brush up on something you learned back in school but have since forgotten.

You can choose to read an Everything® book from cover to cover or just pick out the information you want from our four useful boxes: e-questions, e-facts, e-alerts, and e-ssentials.

We give you everything you need to know on the subject, but throw in a lot of fun stuff along the way, too.

We now have more than 400 Everything® books in print, spanning such wide-ranging categories as weddings, pregnancy, cooking, music instruction, foreign language, crafts, pets, New Age, and so much more. When you're done reading them all, you can finally say you know Everything®!

QUESTION

Answers to
common questions

FACT

Important snippets
of information

ALERT

Urgent
warnings

ESSENTIAL

Quick
handy tips

PUBLISHER Karen Cooper

DIRECTOR OF ACQUISITIONS AND INNOVATION Paula Munier

MANAGING EDITOR, EVERYTHING® SERIES Lisa Laing

COPY CHIEF Casey Ebert

ASSISTANT PRODUCTION EDITOR Melanie Cordova

ACQUISITIONS EDITOR Lisa Laing

SENIOR DEVELOPMENT EDITOR Brett Palana-Shanahan

EDITORIAL ASSISTANT Ross Weisman

NUTRITIONAL ANALYSIS Nicóle Cormier, RD

EVERYTHING® SERIES COVER DESIGNER Erin Alexander

LAYOUT DESIGNERS Erin Dawson, Michelle Roy Kelly, Elisabeth Lariviere, Denise Wallace

Visit the entire Everything® series at www.everything.com

THE EVERYTHING® VEGETARIAN SLOW COOKER COOKBOOK

Amy Snyder and Justin Snyder

Adamsmedia
Avon, Massachusetts

An Everything® Series Book.
Everything® and everything.com® are registered trademarks of F+W Media, Inc.

Published by Adams Media, a division of F+W Media, Inc.
57 Littlefield Street, Avon, MA 02322 U.S.A.
www.adamsmedia.com

ISBN 10: 1-4405-2858-6
ISBN 13: 978-1-4405-2858-3
eISBN 10: 1-4405-2928-0
eISBN 13: 978-1-4405-2928-3

Printed in the United States of America.

10 9 8 7 6 5 4 3

Library of Congress Cataloging-in-Publication Data
is available from the publisher.

This publication is designed to provide accurate and authoritative information with regard to the subject matter covered. It is sold with the understanding that the publisher is not engaged in rendering legal, accounting, or other professional advice. If legal advice or other expert assistance is required, the services of a competent professional person should be sought.

—From a *Declaration of Principles* jointly adopted by a Committee of the American Bar Association and a Committee of Publishers and Associations

Many of the designations used by manufacturers and sellers to distinguish their products are claimed as trademarks. Where those designations appear in this book and Adams Media was aware of a trademark claim, the designations have been printed with initial capital letters.

This book is available at quantity discounts for bulk purchases.
For information, please call 1-800-289-0963.

Contents

Introduction

GONE ARE THE DAYS when being a vegetarian or vegan meant the most exciting thing you ate was brown rice and plain tofu. These days, meat-free recipes are anything but boring because cooks aren't afraid to load them with flavor that comes from an array of herbs, spices, exotic ingredients, and more common ingredients that are now used in new and interesting ways. Vegetarian and vegan diets—a diet that is completely free of animal products, including meat, eggs, dairy, and honey—no longer make you think of everything you *can't* eat and instead open the door to all of the delicious foods you may have once ignored. The availability of mouthwatering meat-free recipes, the abundance of prepared vegetarian items in national grocery store chains and at restaurants, and the wealth of information about the health and environmental benefits of a humane diet mean that this way of eating is on the rise. Luckily, this book will arm you with 300 slow cooker recipes that can all be made vegetarian or vegan—it's up to you!

Slow cookers, too, have been gaining in popularity recently because they are must-have time savers for busy families. One of the greatest benefits of slow cooking is that after you have completed the initial preparation for a recipe, you don't have to stay in the kitchen to watch and stir what's cooking away in the slow cooker. When using a slow cooker, you can put your ingredients over low heat, cover the pot, and go. Hours later when you return, your dinner is served and no one will be able to tell you didn't spend hours in the kitchen. Slow cooking is truly a no-fuss cooking method that should be employed by all home cooks.

The slow cooking method is especially ideal for the vegetarian staples—beans, tempeh, and seitan. Tempeh is made from fermented soy beans and seitan is made from the gluten of wheat. Both are used to replace meat in many recipes—such as using shredded seitan in place of chicken or using crumbled tempeh instead of beef—and are an excellent source of vegetarian protein. Unfortunately, these wonderful ingredients can be a little tough if not cooked properly, and they benefit from a long cooking time while immersed in liquid so that it may tenderize the proteins and help them absorb flavors, which they don't do easily. That is where a slow cooker comes in. The slow cooker is the perfect kitchen tool for safely cooking vegetarian staples for long periods of time in order to bring out the best flavor and texture they have to offer.

This book features 300 recipes for everyday meals and every appetite. Browse through each chapter and you will see recipes from Asia, India, Africa, Europe, and from just about every part of North America. Whether you're vegan, vegetarian, or a meat eater, these global recipes offer something for everyone. Even better, they can easily be altered to please a variety of taste buds. Unlike other cooking methods such as baking or pressure cooking, slow cooking is less of an exact science, and you shouldn't fear "messing it up." It's okay to substitute ingredients or just leave out the ones you don't like, as long as you always cook each recipe with enough liquid to make the slow cooker function properly. So, give vegetarian slow cooking a try, but remember to experiment, eat, and enjoy!

Note: When any of the recipes in this book gives an optional ingredient choice, for example "butter or vegan margarine," the nutritional information is calculated using the first option.

CHAPTER 1

An Introduction to Slow Cookers and Vegetarianism

If you're looking for a healthier way of eating and a time-saving method of cooking homemade meals, vegetarian slow cooking is for you. Vegetarian diets are typically lower in saturated fat and cholesterol than standard diets, and vegan diets are naturally cholesterol free. But when you prepare vegetarian meals in a slow cooker you won't just be improving your health, you'll use less electricity than an oven and you'll save yourself time, making the combination of vegetarianism and a slow cooker a win-win for you and your family.

Why Slow Cookers?

Slow cookers are affordable, easy to use, and fit conveniently on your counter top. After cooking a meal, you can easily remove the pot to clean it and the slow cooker lid in a dishwasher or by hand. Surprisingly, though, these aren't even the best reasons to choose a slow cooker for making your meals. The main reasons why slow cookers are a great choice for preparing delicious vegetarian recipes is because they're convenient, they save energy, and they are excellent at breaking down tough proteins.

Convenience

There are several benefits to slow cooking, but the one that is probably the most commonly cited is convenience. Many slow cooker recipes call for a long cooking time, and the appliance does not require constant supervision, which frees you to complete other tasks or even go to work while the meal is cooking. For busy parents, the appliance can be a time and life saver.

ALERT

All slow cookers are unique and come with their own set of instructions and warnings. Recommendations may be different based on the brand and size of the slow cooker. Be sure to read the information provided with your slow cooker carefully before getting started.

Slow cooking is done at a lower temperature than most other methods of preparation, which means recipes require a longer cooking time. Most slow cooker recipes also call for covering the pot with a lid, which means that liquid will not escape, and eliminates the risk of burning your food. Locking in the moisture this way means that you don't have to constantly monitor your food, as you would with stovetop cooking.

Energy Saver

When using a slow cooker, the energy saved is not just your own! This countertop appliance actually uses less electricity than an oven when preparing most recipes, and by reducing the energy used for cooking meals a few days a week, your kitchen will be a little greener. Using less electricity means your wallet may end up being a little heavier, too, because of the savings you'll see on your utilities.

Tough Stuff

Slow cookers are often used to prepare recipes that call for cheaper cuts of meat because the longer cooking time helps soften the meat. While vegetarians don't eat meat, they can apply this information to cooking their protein staples: beans, tempeh, and seitan.

QUESTION

Can I cook dried beans in a slow cooker?
Dried beans may be prepared in a slow cooker, but you must first soak them overnight and boil the beans for 10 minutes before using them in recipes in order to remove the toxins found in some beans. This adds a fair amount of time to each recipe, so canned beans are often recommended instead.

Most slow cooker recipes call for enough liquid to submerge the main ingredients, and a long cooking time. Soaking tempeh in a warm liquid for such an extended period of time helps soften and break down the dense protein made of fermented soybeans. Seitan isn't nearly as dense as tempeh, but it's also not very good at absorbing flavor, and slow cooking helps overcome this "wheat meat" obstacle.

Slow Cooking Tips and Tricks

Slow cookers are easy to use, but that doesn't mean a few tips and tricks won't help you achieve optimal results. And even a slow cooker veteran can use some handy reminders before firing up the slow cooker again. Here are a few tips and tricks to help you out.

- Recipes that call for a large quantity of liquid work best.
- The pot in your slow cooker should never be less than half full.

- The high setting is the same temperature as the low setting, food just reaches the simmer point faster.
- The lid should be used when operating a slow cooker.
- Stirring food during cooking is unnecessary.

As with any method of cooking, you won't find out what works best for your recipes until you try it out yourself. Use these tips to get you started or to help you troubleshoot problems you may be having with your slow cooker, and if they continue, contact the manufacturer or try an Internet search to solve the problem. If all else fails, try the recipe again!

Adapting Recipes for Your Slow Cooker

Many recipes that were originally designed for an oven or stovetop can easily be adapted for just about any slow cooker. The main principles of slow cooking are that you cook ingredients in liquid, covered, for a long period of time. As long as you keep this in mind, you shouldn't be afraid to experiment with other recipes that were not originally intended for a slow cooker.

Some cooking methods are easier to adapt for a slow cooker than others, though. For example, don't attempt to deep-fry food in a slow cooker on the low setting because the oil will not be hot enough to cook your food in a desirable way. Methods that call for cooking in a liquid, such as braising and stewing, are easiest for adapting to a slow cooker.

ESSENTIAL

Whether you are cooking food in a slow cooker, the oven, or on the stove, the flavor of food will remain largely the same. Some methods highlight ingredients better than others, but for the most part, flavors don't change. Remember this when adapting recipes for your slow cooker.

Slow cookers don't require exact cooking times or ingredient measurements like baking does, which means you shouldn't be afraid to experiment! As long as you follow your slow cooker's instructions and use enough liquid to prevent burning, you're free to mix and match ingredients until you create recipes that work perfectly for your palette. If a recipe calls for basil but you're not a fan of the herb, try substituting oregano or thyme instead. If you've never tried tofu, tempeh, or seitan, add them to your favorite recipe to try out their interesting texture and get a vegetarian protein punch.

Vegetarian 101

A vegetarian is usually defined as one who does not consume animal flesh, including fish and other seafood. Most people who refer to themselves as vegetarian do eat eggs and dairy products, and may still wear animal products such as fur, leather, and wool. Those who take their stance against cruelty to animals a step further and avoid all animal products, including meat, eggs, dairy, and honey, are called vegans. In many cases, this lifestyle choice does not apply only to food but is also reflected in their choice of clothing, makeup, and household products. In most cases, vegans try to live a 100 percent cruelty-free lifestyle.

Vegetarianism and veganism are rapidly gaining in popularity across the United States, but the reason for going meat free varies greatly from person to person. For some, the decision is reached after watching graphic footage of how animals are housed and then slaughtered on modern factory farms and in slaughterhouses. Some people realize that they can no longer contribute to the routine cruelty they've witnessed. The decision may be based on the many health benefits of choosing a meat-free diet or the desire to try to undo the environmental harm caused by the meat industry. For others, the decision may be based on religion, upbringing, or other personal factors.

FACT

Eating meat means wasting an essential resource—water. The average vegetarian diet takes 300 gallons of water per day to produce, while the average meat-filled diet takes more than 4,000 gallons of water to produce.

Finding the ingredients to help you fuel your vegetarian or vegan diet is now easier than ever before. Many national grocery store chains carry popular mock meats, such as the Boca and Morningstar Farms brands. Several even have health food sections that are stocked with vegan mayonnaise, tofu, and soymilk. Better yet, many of the products sitting in your cupboards right now might be "accidentally vegan." Popular items such as Bisquick, some Duncan Hines cake mixes, and even some flavors of Jell-O brand instant pudding are all vegan if you prepare them with vegan products. For those items that aren't quite as easy to find, try searching online for vegan retailers.

In addition to online vegan specialty stores that sell food products, there are a multitude of other resources online that will help with your transition to a vegetarian or vegan diet. Groups such as People for the Ethical Treatment of Animals (PETA) offer free vegetarian starter kits, recipes, lists of "accidentally vegan" food items, information on animal rights, and much more.

Vegetarian Nutrition

What do vegans eat? Where do vegetarians get their protein? Are you worried about becoming anemic? These are common questions many vegans and vegetarians face, but they are largely unfounded. Vegan and vegetarian diets are loaded with essential nutrients and, if done right, can be healthier than a diet full of meat and cheese. Like with any diet, the key is to choose healthful foods and limit your consumption of fatty, sugar- or sodium-heavy, and overly processed foods to a minimum. When choosing the healthiest foods the majority of the time, vegan and vegetarian diets can be full of protein, iron, calcium, and other vital nutrients.

Protein

Protein is a required nutrient for maintaining a healthy body. Luckily, many foods considered the staple of a meat-free diet are rich with protein, without containing any of the fat and cholesterol found in meat. The real protein powerhouse is the soybean. This powerful bean contains a whopping 28.62 grams of protein per cup. Soybeans are commonly used in mock meats and vegan dairy products, but they can also be cooked and prepared in other recipes, so getting your daily requirement of protein should not be a problem if soy is a part of your plan.

▼ HEALTHY PROTEIN SOURCES

Ingredient	Grams of Protein
Soybeans, boiled (1 cup)	28.62
Lentils, boiled (1 cup)	17.9
Pinto beans, boiled (1 cup)	15.4
Black beans, boiled (1 cup)	15.2
Chickpeas, boiled (1 cup)	14.5
Soymilk, unfortified (1 cup)	8.0
Roasted peanuts (1 ounce)	8.0
Spinach, boiled (1 cup)	7.6
Couscous, cooked (1 cup)	6.0
Broccoli, cooked (1 cup)	5.7
Whole-wheat bread (1 slice)	4.1

Source: USDA.gov

Another benefit to consuming plant-based proteins over animal proteins is that these ingredients typically contain fiber and complex carbohydrates that are not found in animal products. For example, lentils, which contain 17.9 grams of protein per cup, also contain 15.6 grams of fiber!

Iron

Anemia, which can be caused by iron deficiency, is a common concern of some new vegans and vegetarians. People worry that if they leave meat off their plate, they won't be able to reach the daily recommended intake. However, a study in the *American Journal of Clinical Nutrition* states that there is no significant difference in anemia levels between vegetarians and meat eaters. Vegetarian foods are loaded with iron, and according to the USDA's National Nutrient Database, some of the most iron-rich foods are vegetarian. Several cereals top the USDA's list, along with Cream of Wheat, soybeans, some canned beans, lentils, and more. Iron deficiency is a very real concern, but not more so for vegetarians and vegans than for meat eaters.

Calcium

Cows produce milk to nourish their young and provide all of the nutrients they need to grow strong, just as humans do. But no species drink the milk of another species—except humans. Humans consume cow's milk throughout their lifetime, even though it is the number one cause of food allergies in infants and children, and millions of people around the world suffer from lactose intolerance. Many plant-based foods are an alternative source of calcium that don't come with the health problems associated with drinking cow's milk. Many soymilks and brands of orange juice are fortified with calcium, but it is also found naturally in several items. Collard greens, rhubarb, spinach, and soybeans are just a few of the rich sources of plant-based calcium.

ESSENTIAL

As with any diet, eating a variety of fresh and healthy foods is the key to optimal nutrition. Vegetarians should focus on consuming a variety of whole foods such as beans, nuts, whole grains, fruits, and vegetables. This, paired with supplements for any vitamins you may be missing, will put you one step closer to a healthier you.

Protein, iron, and calcium are just some of the nutrients you find naturally in vegan and vegetarian foods, but there are a couple that may be best consumed through a supplement or other method. For example, you may prefer to get your daily dose of vitamin D from basking in the sun, but you can also get it through items such as fortified soymilk. However, vitamin B_{12} is not found naturally in plant-based foods, and must be obtained through a supplement such as a multivitamin. Just be sure to read the label and make sure it contains B_{12}.

Adapting Recipes for Your Vegetarian Diet

As with adapting recipes for your slow cooker, adapting recipes for your vegan or vegetarian diet can be easy, healthy, and tasty. Some adaptations will include replacing an animal product with a cruelty-free alternative, but others will involve finding a new and exciting approach to food. Instead of always trying to find a way to make your dish taste as if it contains meat, dairy, or eggs, there are many ways for adding rich flavors. Use these four tips to get started.

Know Your Cooking Times

Faux meats and soy cheeses may offer flavors similar to animal products, but they are very different than the real thing. Many mock meats require a much shorter cooking time than animal flesh; conversely, vegan cheeses may take much longer to melt. When replacing the flesh or by-product of an animal with a cruelty-free version, remember to read the package instructions and adjust your cooking times accordingly.

Some Techniques Should Be Avoided

When reading the packaging for many faux meats, you will also find that certain techniques for preparation should be avoided. Some brands of veggie hot dogs or sausages can be prepared on the open flame of a grill, but not all. Cooking on a grill may lead to an overly done and tough veggie dog. For others, baking in the oven may not lead to optimal results. Be sure to read the package instructions before proceeding.

Flavors Don't (Have to) Change

If you are replacing chicken flesh with a vegan product, such as Morningstar Farms Meal Starter Chik'n Strips, you can build the flavors in your recipe around it just as you would real chicken. The accompanying flavors in your recipe do not need to be adjusted just because you're ditching the meat. You can, however, take this opportunity to explore a diverse world of new flavors. A meal does not have to be centered around meat for the protein—beans, tempeh, and tofu are great alternatives that are rich in protein and will bring new tastes and textures to your cooking.

One of the best parts of trying a new diet is that you get to experiment with new recipes and foods! Ethnic cuisines such as Indian, Japanese, and Middle Eastern can be more vegetarian friendly than traditional American fare because of the diverse proteins used in their recipes. Experiment with recipes from around the world to find your favorites, or experiment with "veganizing" your family's favorite recipes.

Experiment

Finding vegetarian and vegan versions of your favorite products is easier than ever before; just check out all of the options at your local grocery store or natural health food store. For any products that are hard to find in your area, try ordering online. Refer to Appendix C for a listing of online stores. And for more information on how to replace specific animal products in your recipes, see Appendix B for a list of common substitutions.

CHAPTER 2

Appetizers and Snacks

Spicy Buffalo Strips

*Most bottled buffalo wing sauces contain butter, so if you're vegan,
make your own by following the steps below.*

INGREDIENTS | SERVES 6

⅓ cup butter or vegan margarine
⅓ cup hot sauce
1 tablespoon vinegar
1 teaspoon garlic powder
2 (7-ounce) packages Gardein Chick'n
Strips

Serving Strips

Faux buffalo chicken strips can be added
to sandwiches or salads, but if you'd like to
serve them as an appetizer or snack, place
in a small basket lined with parchment
paper and add sides of celery sticks, carrot
sticks, and vegan ranch.

1. Place the butter or margarine in a small bowl and microwave for 30 seconds, or until melted.

2. Add the hot sauce, vinegar, and garlic powder and stir well.

3. In a 4-quart slow cooker, add the prepared hot sauce and Chick'n Strips and cook over low heat for 1 hour.

PER SERVING Calories: 187 | Fat: 10 g | Protein: 17 g | Sodium: 566 mg | Fiber: 1 g | Carbohydrates: 8 g | Sugar: 0 g

Baba Gannouj

Serve with toasted pita chips or as a vegetable dip.

INGREDIENTS | YIELDS 1½ CUPS

1 tablespoon olive oil
1 large eggplant, peeled and diced
4 cloves garlic, peeled and minced
½ cup water
3 tablespoons fresh parsley
½ teaspoon salt
2 tablespoons fresh lemon juice
2 tablespoons tahini
1 tablespoon extra-virgin olive oil

1. In a 4-quart slow cooker, add the olive oil, eggplant, garlic, and water and stir until coated. Cover and cook on high heat for 4 hours.

2. Strain the cooked eggplant and garlic and add to a food processor or blender along with the parsley, salt, lemon juice, and tahini. Pulse to process.

3. Scrape down the side of the food processor or blender container if necessary. Add the extra virgin olive oil and process until smooth.

PER SERVING (½ CUP) Calories: 24 | Fat: 2 g | Protein: 0.5 g | Sodium: 52 mg | Fiber: 1 g | Carbohydrates: 2 g | Sugar: 0.5 g

Chili-Cheese Dip

The perfect accompaniment for this dip is salty corn tortilla chips.

INGREDIENTS | SERVES 12

1 (15-ounce) can vegetarian chili
¼ cup diced onions
½ cup diced tomatoes
1 (8-ounce) package cream cheese or vegan cream cheese
1 cup Cheddar cheese or vegan Cheddar
1 teaspoon garlic powder

1. In a 4-quart slow cooker, place all ingredients.

2. Stir gently; cover, and heat on low for 1 hour.

PER SERVING Calories: 163 | Fat: 13 g | Protein: 6 g | Sodium: 296 mg | Fiber: 1 g | Carbohydrates: 6 g | Sugar: 1.5 g

Vegetarian Chili

Most major grocery stores sell canned vegetarian chili. One of the easiest to find is Hormel's Vegetarian Chili with Beans, which contains textured vegetable protein instead of meat.

Teriyaki "Chicken" Strips

Any brand of vegan or vegetarian chicken strips will work in this recipe.

INGREDIENTS | SERVES 6

2 (7-ounce) packages Gardein Chick'n Strips
5–6 ounces teriyaki sauce
1 teaspoon hot sauce

1. In a 4-quart slow cooker, combine all ingredients and cook over low heat for 1 hour.

PER SERVING Calories: 86 | Fat: 0 g | Protein: 16 g | Sodium: 1,078 mg | Fiber: 1 g | Carbohydrates: 9 g | Sugar: 3 g

Broccoli Dip

Serve this vegetable-rich creamy dip with crisp raw vegetables and pumpernickel pretzels.

INGREDIENTS | SERVES 15

4 cups steamed broccoli florets

1 cup fresh baby spinach

1 shallot

1 jalapeño, stem and seeds removed

1 tablespoon vegan Worcestershire sauce

½ tablespoon nonpareil capers

8 ounces cream cheese or vegan cream cheese

8 ounces sour cream or vegan sour cream

¼ teaspoon freshly ground black pepper

2 tablespoons lemon juice

1. In a food processor, place the broccoli, spinach, shallot, jalapeño, Worcestershire sauce, and capers. Pulse until the mixture is mostly smooth.

2. Add the cream cheese, sour cream, pepper, and lemon juice. Pulse until smooth.

3. Pour into a 1½- or 2-quart slow cooker. Cover and cook on low for 1 hour.

PER SERVING Calories: 90 | Fat: 8 g | Protein: 2 g | Sodium: 90 mg | Fiber: 0.5 g | Carbohydrates: 3 g | Sugar: 2 g

How to Steam Vegetables

Bring about 1" of water to boil in a heavy-bottomed pot. Add the vegetables and cook until fork-tender but not soft. Drain and season.

Cajun Peanuts

Use "green" raw peanuts, not cooked or dried nuts.

INGREDIENTS | SERVES 16

2 pounds raw peanuts

12 cups water

⅓ cup salt

1 (3-ounce) package crab boil

1. Rinse the peanuts under cold water, then place in a 6-quart slow cooker.

2. Add the water, salt and crab boil, cover and cook on high for 7 hours.

PER SERVING Calories: 317 | Fat: 28 g | Protein: 14 g | Sodium: 2,373 mg | Fiber: 5 g | Carbohydrates: 9 g | Sugar: 2 g

Barbecue "Meatballs"

Enjoy these "meatballs" as a two-bite snack or use them as the filling in a hearty sub.

INGREDIENTS | YIELDS 12 "MEATBALLS"

1 pound vegetarian ground beef, such as Gimme Lean Beef

½ onion, diced

1 clove garlic, minced

½ cup panko bread crumbs

1 (18-ounce) bottle barbecue sauce

Panko Bread Crumbs

Panko is a type of bread crumb made from white bread without crusts. It typically creates a crispier texture when used as the coating on food than regular bread crumbs. To make your own, bake crustless white bread crumbs until they are dry, but not browned.

1. In a large mixing bowl, combine the vegetarian ground beef, onion, garlic, and bread crumbs, and mix until well combined. (Using your hands is the easiest method.) Roll the "beef" mixture into 12 meatballs.

2. To a 4-quart slow cooker, add the "meatballs."

3. Cover with barbecue sauce. Cover and cook over high heat for 1 hour.

PER SERVING (2 "MEATBALLS") Calories: 268 | Fat: 4.5 g | Protein: 17 g | Sodium: 1056 mg | Fiber: 1 g | Carbohydrates: 38 g | Sugar: 23 g

Frijole Dip

For best results, serve this dip immediately after cooking or reheat if it cools.

INGREDIENTS | SERVES 12

2 (15-ounce) cans pinto beans, drained

1½ cups water

1 tablespoon olive oil

1 small onion, peeled and diced

3 cloves garlic, peeled and minced

1 cup diced tomato

1 teaspoon chipotle powder

½ teaspoon cumin

¼ cup fresh cilantro, finely chopped

Salt, to taste

1 cup Monterey jack cheese, grated, or vegan Monterey jack cheese

1. In a 4-quart slow cooker, add the beans, water, olive oil, onion, and garlic. Cover and cook over low heat for 1 hour.

2. Mash the beans until about ½ are smooth and ½ are still chunky.

3. Add all remaining ingredients; stir well, and cook for an additional 30 minutes.

PER SERVING Calories: 66 | Fat: 2 g | Protein: 4 g | Sodium: 172 mg | Fiber: 2 g | Carbohydrates: 8 g | Sugar: 1 g

Vegan Spinach and Artichoke Dip

Serve with toasted pita points or slices of warm baguette.

INGREDIENTS | YIELDS 4 CUPS

1 (15-ounce) can artichokes, drained and chopped

2 cups water

1 teaspoon lemon juice

1 tablespoon vegan margarine, such as Earth Balance

1 cup thawed frozen spinach, chopped

8 ounces vegan cream cheese, such as Tofutti Better Than Cream Cheese

16 ounces vegan sour cream, such as Tofutti Sour Supreme

⅓ cup vegan Parmesan cheese

¼ teaspoon garlic powder

¼ teaspoon salt

In a 4-quart slow cooker, add all ingredients. Cover and cook over low heat for 1 hour.

PER SERVING (¼ CUP) Calories: 177 | Fat: 16 g | Protein: 5 g | Sodium: 244 mg | Fiber: 2 g | Carbohydrates: 6 g | Sugar: 2 g

Serving Options

This recipe calls for serving the dip warm, but chilling the dip and serving cool is also delicious. After cooking, let the dip cool to room temperature and store in the refrigerator in an airtight container. Let cool for at least 3 hours before serving.

Cinnamon and Sugar Peanuts

This is a festive treat that can be packaged in cellophane bags and given as party favors or gifts.

INGREDIENTS | YIELDS 12 OUNCES

12 ounces unsalted, roasted peanuts
½ tablespoon ground cinnamon
⅓ cup sugar
1 tablespoon melted butter or vegan margarine

1. In a 4-quart slow cooker, place the peanuts.

2. Add the cinnamon and sugar and drizzle with butter. Stir.

3. Cook on low, uncovered, for 2–3 hours, stirring occasionally.

4. Spread the peanut mixture onto a cookie sheet or parchment paper and cool until dry.

PER SERVING (1 OUNCE) Calories: 200 | Fat: 15 g | Protein: 7 g | Sodium: 0 mg | Fiber: 2 g | Carbohydrates: 12 g | Sugar: 7 g

Caramelized Onion Dip

Caramelized onions give this dip an amazing depth of flavor.

**INGREDIENTS | YIELDS 1 QUART
(32 SERVINGS)**

⅔ cup Caramelized Onions (see Chapter 7)

8 ounces reduced-fat cream cheese

8 ounces reduced-fat sour cream

1 tablespoon vegan Worcestershire sauce

¼ teaspoon white pepper

⅛ teaspoon flour

1. Place all ingredients into a 1½- to 2-quart slow cooker.

2. Heat on low for 2 hours. Whisk before serving.

PER SERVING (2 TABLESPOONS) Calories: 30 | Fat: 1.5 g | Protein: 1 g | Sodium: 35 mg | Fiber: 0 g | Carbohydrates: 3 g | Sugar: 1 g

Make It Vegan

Make this recipe vegan by using Toffuti Better Than Cream Cheese (vegan cream cheese) and Tofutti Sour Supreme (vegan sour cream) instead of the dairy versions.

Zesty Lemon Hummus

Serve this Middle Eastern spread with pita, vegetables, or falafel.

INGREDIENTS | SERVES 20

1 pound dried chickpeas
Water, as needed
3 tablespoons tahini
4 tablespoons lemon juice
Zest of 1 lemon
3 cloves garlic
¼ teaspoon salt

Easy Snacking

Keeping hummus and fresh vegetables around makes healthy snacking easy. Cut carrots, celery, and radishes into snack-friendly sizes. Place them in a bowl with a tightly fitting lid. Fill the bowl ⅔ with water. They will keep crisp in the refrigerator up to 1 week.

1. In a 4-quart slow cooker, place the chickpeas and cover with water. Soak overnight, drain, and rinse. The next day, cook on low for 8 hours. Drain, reserving the liquid.

2. In a food processor, place the chickpeas, tahini, lemon juice, lemon zest, garlic, and salt. Pulse until smooth, adding the reserved liquid as needed to achieve the desired texture.

PER SERVING Calories: 97 | Fat: 2.5 g | Protein: 5 g | Sodium: 38 mg | Fiber: 4 g | Carbohydrates: 15 g | Sugar: 2.5 g

Mixed Veggie Dip

Try this vegetable-rich dip with pita chips or baked potato chips.

INGREDIENTS | SERVES 20

8 ounces low-fat cream cheese, room temperature

½ cup reduced-fat sour cream

1 teaspoon low-fat mayonnaise

½ teaspoon white pepper

½ teaspoon garlic powder

½ teaspoon onion powder

½ teaspoon vegan Worcestershire sauce

1 carrot, minced

1 stalk celery, minced

3 tablespoons fresh spinach, minced

¼ cup broccoli, minced

1. In a 2-quart slow cooker, thoroughly mix all ingredients.

2. Cook on low for 2 hours. Stir before serving.

PER SERVING Calories: 40 | Fat: 3 g | Protein: 2 g | Sodium: 45 mg | Fiber: 0 g | Carbohydrates: 2 g | Sugar: 1 g

Make It Vegan

Make this recipe vegan by using Toffuti Better Than Cream Cheese (vegan cream cheese), Tofutti Sour Supreme (vegan sour cream), and Vegenaise (vegan mayonnaise) instead of the dairy-filled versions.

Summer Fruit Dip

Kiwi, strawberries, star fruit, banana, and citrus are all excellent dipping choices for this fruity dip, which is also delicious served cold.

INGREDIENTS | SERVES 20

½ cup raspberry purée

8 ounces reduced-fat cream cheese or vegan cream cheese, room temperature

1 tablespoon sugar

¾ cup reduced-fat sour cream or vegan sour cream

1 teaspoon vanilla

1. In a small bowl, whisk together all ingredients.

2. Pour into a 2-quart slow cooker; cook on low for 1 hour. Stir before serving.

PER SERVING Calories: 55 | Fat: 5 g | Protein: 1 g | Sodium: 40 mg | Fiber: 0 g | Carbohydrates: 2.1 g | Sugar: 1.5 g

Sun-Dried Tomato Pesto Dip

*Tart, rich sun-dried tomatoes are the perfect partner
for a fresh-tasting pesto in this creamy dip.*

INGREDIENTS | SERVES 20

2 cloves garlic

1 tablespoon reduced-fat mayonnaise or Vegenaise

¾ ounce fresh basil

1 teaspoon toasted pine nuts

¼ teaspoon white pepper

¼ cup dry (not oil-packed) sun-dried tomatoes, julienne cut

8 ounces reduced-fat cream cheese or vegan cream cheese, room temperature

1. In a food processor, place the garlic, mayonnaise or Vegenaise, basil, pine nuts, and pepper. Pulse until a fairly smooth paste forms.

2. Add the sun-dried tomatoes and pulse 4–5 times.

3. Add the cream cheese and pulse until smooth.

4. Scrape into a 2-quart slow cooker. Cook on low for 1 hour. Stir before serving.

PER SERVING Calories: 35 | Fat: 3 g | Protein: 1 g | Sodium: 65 mg | Fiber: 0 g | Carbohydrates: 1 g | Sugar: 0.5 g

How to Toast Pine Nuts

Preheat the oven to 350°F. Place the pine nuts on a cookie sheet or cake pan. Roast for 5–8 minutes in the oven. Pine nuts will be slightly browned and fragrant when fully toasted. Cool before using.

CHAPTER 3

Soups

Vegetable Broth

A versatile vegetable broth can be used as the base for almost any soup or stew.
Note that it does not contain salt, so you must add that separately when using this broth in recipes.

INGREDIENTS | YIELDS 4 CUPS

2 large onions, peeled and halved

2 medium carrots, cleaned and cut into large pieces

3 stalks celery, cut in half

1 whole bulb garlic, crushed

10 peppercorns

1 bay leaf

6 cups water

1. In a 4-quart slow cooker, add all ingredients. Cover and cook on low heat for 8–10 hours.

2. Strain the broth to remove the vegetables. Store broth in the refrigerator.

PER SERVING (1 CUP) Calories: 42 | Fat: 0 g | Protein: 1 g | Sodium: 62 | Fiber: 2 g | Carbohydrates: 9.5 g | Sugar: 4.5 g

Storing Broth

Homemade broth can be stored in a covered container in the refrigerator for 2–3 days, or frozen for up to 3 months.

No-Beef Broth

Traditional Worcestershire sauce contains anchovies,
but several grocery store brands of the sauce are vegan.

INGREDIENTS | YIELDS 4 CUPS

4 carrots, washed and cut into large pieces

2 large onions, peeled and quartered

1 celery stalk, chopped

2 cups fresh portobello mushrooms, sliced

1 whole bulb garlic, crushed

1 tablespoon vegan Worcestershire sauce

1 tablespoon brown sugar

6 cups water

1. In a 4-quart slow cooker, add all ingredients. Cover, and cook on low heat for 8–10 hours.

2. Strain the broth to remove the vegetables. Store the broth in a covered container in the refrigerator for 2–3 days, or frozen for up to 3 months.

PER SERVING (1 CUP) Calories: 90 | Fat: 0 g | Protein: 3 g | Sodium: 108 mg | Fiber: 4 g | Carbohydrates: 21 g | Sugar: 11 g

Tofu Noodle Soup

For added texture, freeze the tofu and bake before adding to the soup.

INGREDIENTS | SERVES 4

2 tablespoons olive oil

1 medium onion, diced

3 cloves garlic, minced

2 ribs celery, sliced in ½" pieces

7 ounces extra-firm tofu, cubed

5 cups Vegetable Broth (see recipe in this chapter)

1 bay leaf

1 teaspoon salt

Juice of 1 lemon

2 teaspoons fresh parsley, chopped

2 teaspoons fresh thyme, chopped

8 ounces cooked egg noodles or linguine

1. In a large sauté pan heat the olive oil over medium heat. Add the onion, garlic, and celery and sauté for 3 minutes.

2. Add the tofu and cook 5 additional minutes.

3. In a 4-quart slow cooker, pour the sautéed vegetables, tofu, Vegetable Broth, bay leaf, and salt. Cover, and cook on low for 8 hours.

4. Add the lemon juice, parsley, thyme and pasta. Cover and cook for an additional 20 minutes.

PER SERVING Calories: 401 | Fat: 9 g | Protein: 14 g | Sodium: 805 mg | Fiber: 9 g | Carbohydrates: 66 g | Sugar: 13 g

Herbal Options

A variety of herbs can work well in Tofu Noodle Soup. Try substituting basil, rosemary, or even dill in this recipe.

Hot and Sour Soup

Adjust the spiciness of this soup by adding more or less chili paste, to taste.

INGREDIENTS | SERVES 6

4 cups Vegetable Broth (see recipe in this chapter)

2 tablespoons soy sauce

2 tablespoons rice vinegar

1 teaspoon sesame oil

2 ounces dried Chinese mushrooms

½ cup canned bamboo shoots, sliced

4 ounces extra-firm tofu, cubed

1 tablespoon red chili paste

1 teaspoon white pepper

2 tablespoons cornstarch mixed with ¼ cup water

1. In a 4-quart slow cooker, add all ingredients except for the cornstarch mixture; cook on low for 6 hours.

2. Pour in the cornstarch mixture; stir, and cook on high heat for 20 additional minutes.

PER SERVING Calories: 76 | Fat: 1.5 g | Protein: 3 g | Sodium: 397 mg | Fiber: 3 g | Carbohydrates: 13 g | Sugar: 5 g

Cauliflower Soup

Cauliflower's peak season is the fall, so try this soup on a crisp autumn night.

INGREDIENTS | SERVES 6

1 small head cauliflower, chopped

½ onion, diced

1 teaspoon salt

1 teaspoon pepper

2 tablespoons butter or vegan margarine

4 cups Vegetable Broth (see recipe in this chapter)

Zest of ½ lemon

1. In a 4-quart slow cooker, add all ingredients. Cover, and cook on low for 6 hours.

2. Turn off slow cooker and let soup cool about 10 minutes. Using a blender or immersion blender, process until very smooth.

3. Return soup to the slow cooker; add lemon zest, and heat until warm.

PER SERVING Calories: 98 | Fat: 4 g | Protein: 3 g | Sodium: 474 mg | Fiber: 4 g | Carbohydrates: 14 g | Sugar: 6 g

Zest Versus Juice

Lemon zest is obtained by grating the outer peel of the lemon. It contains a more intense lemon flavor than the juice of the citrus fruit, although many recipes call for both lemon zest and lemon juice.

White Bean and Barley Soup

Cool soup to room temperature before refrigerating or freezing in order to save energy.

INGREDIENTS | SERVES 8

2 (15-ounce) cans great northern beans, drained and rinsed

½ cup pearl barley

½ onion, diced

2 carrots, peeled and diced

2 cloves garlic, minced

¼ cup fresh parsley, chopped

2 sprigs fresh thyme

6 cups No-Beef Broth (see recipe in this chapter)

1½ teaspoons salt

1. In a 4-quart slow cooker, add all ingredients. Cover, and cook on low for 6–8 hours.

2. Remove the sprig of thyme before serving.

PER SERVING Calories: 182.5 | Fat: 1 g | Protein: 8 g | Sodium: 826 mg | Fiber: 10.5 g | Carbohydrates: 37 g | Sugar: 7.5 g

Red Lentil Soup

Store-bought vegetable broth or stock typically contains much more sodium than the homemade variety, so adjust salt accordingly.

INGREDIENTS | SERVES 6

2 cups red lentils

3 tablespoons olive oil

1 small onion, sliced

1½ teaspoons fresh ginger, peeled and minced

2 cloves garlic, minced

6 cups Vegetable Broth (see recipe in this chapter)

Juice of 1 lemon

½ teaspoon paprika

1 teaspoon cayenne pepper

1½ teaspoons salt

1. Rinse the lentils carefully and sort through the bunch to remove any dirt or debris.

2. In a sauté pan, heat the olive oil over medium heat, then sauté the onion, ginger, and garlic for 2–3 minutes.

3. In a 4-quart slow cooker, add the sautéed vegetables and all remaining ingredients. Cover, and cook on low for 6–8 hours. Add more salt, if necessary, to taste.

PER SERVING Calories: 296 | Fat: 8 g | Protein: 18 g | Sodium: 279 mg | Fiber: 8 g | Carbohydrates: 54 g | Sugar: 8 g

Black Bean Soup

You can use the leftover green bell pepper, red bell pepper,
and red onion from this recipe to make Fajita Chili (see Chapter 5).

INGREDIENTS | SERVES 6

2 tablespoons olive oil

½ green bell pepper, diced

½ red bell pepper, diced

½ red onion, sliced

2 cloves garlic, minced

2 (15-ounce) cans black beans, drained and rinsed

2 teaspoons cumin, minced

1 teaspoon chipotle powder

1 teaspoon salt

4 cups Vegetable Broth (see recipe in this chapter)

¼ cup cilantro, chopped

1. In a sauté pan, heat the olive oil over medium heat, then sauté the bell peppers, onion, and garlic for 2–3 minutes.

2. In a 4-quart slow cooker, add the sautéed vegetables, black beans, cumin, chipotle powder, salt, and Vegetable Broth. Cover, and cook on low for 6 hours.

3. Let the soup cool slightly, then pour half into a blender. Process until smooth, then pour back into the pot. Add the chopped cilantro, and stir.

PER SERVING Calories: 204 | Fat: 6 g | Protein: 9 g | Sodium: 865 mg | Fiber: 10 g | Carbohydrates: 31 g | Sugar: 7 g

French Onion Soup

Vidalia onions are a sweet variety of onion that work particularly well in French Onion Soup.

INGREDIENTS | SERVES 4

¼ cup olive oil

4 Vidalia onions, sliced

4 cloves garlic, minced

1 tablespoon dried thyme

1 cup red wine

4 cups Vegetable Broth (see recipe in this chapter)

1 teaspoon salt

1 teaspoon pepper

4 slices French bread

4 ounces Swiss cheese, or vegan cheese such as Daiya Mozzarella Style Shreds

1. In a sauté pan, heat the olive oil over medium high heat and cook the onions until golden brown, about 3 minutes. Add the garlic and sauté for 1 minute.

2. In a 4-quart slow cooker, pour the sautéed vegetables, thyme, red wine, Vegetable Broth, salt and pepper. Cover and cook on low heat for 4 hours.

3. While the soup is cooking, preheat the oven to the broiler setting. Lightly toast the slices of French bread.

4. To serve, ladle the soup into a broiler-safe bowl, place a slice of the toasted French bread on top of the soup, put a slice of the Swiss cheese on top of the bread, and place the soup under the broiler until the cheese has melted.

PER SERVING Calories: 471 | Fat: 22 g | Protein: 14 g | Sodium: 936 mg | Fiber: 6 g | Carbohydrates: 45 g | Sugar: 12 g

Garden Vegetable Soup

Leave the skin on the potatoes in this recipe, and others, for a more rustic, richer potato flavor.

INGREDIENTS | SERVES 6

½ red onion, diced

1 small squash, diced

4 red potatoes, quartered

1 cup okra, sliced

1 cup fresh corn

1 cup green beans, cut into ½" pieces

6 cups Vegetable Broth (see recipe in this chapter)

6 ounces diced tomatoes

1½ teaspoons salt

1 teaspoon pepper

In a 4-quart slow cooker, add all ingredients. Cover and cook over low heat for 6–8 hours.

PER SERVING Calories: 202 | Fat: 0.5 g | Protein: 6 g | Sodium: 681 mg | Fiber: 9 g | Carbohydrates: 46 g | Sugar: 11 g

Choosing the Right Broth

In most soup recipes, you can use Vegetable Broth (see recipe in this chapter) or No-Beef Broth (see recipe in this chapter), depending on how rich you would like the flavor to be. For a full-flavored taste, choose No-Beef Broth, but remember to adjust the salt because No-Beef Broth already has sodium from the vegan Worcestershire sauce.

Potato-Leek Soup

If you'd like to omit the alcohol from this recipe, just add another ½ cup of Vegetable Broth.

INGREDIENTS | SERVES 6

2 tablespoons butter or vegan margarine

2 small leeks, chopped (white and light green parts only)

3 large russet potatoes, peeled and diced

4 cups Vegetable Broth (see recipe in this chapter)

½ cup white wine

½ cup water

1 teaspoon salt

1 teaspoon pepper

¼ teaspoon dried thyme

1. In a sauté pan over medium heat, melt the butter or vegan margarine, then add the leeks. Cook until softened, about 5 minutes.

2. In a 4-quart slow cooker, add the sautéed leeks, potatoes, broth, wine, water, salt, pepper, and thyme. Cover and cook over low heat 6–8 hours.

3. Allow soup to cool slightly, then use an immersion blender or traditional blender to process until smooth.

PER SERVING Calories: 177 | Fat: 4 g | Protein: 3 g | Sodium: 459 mg | Fiber: 5 g | Carbohydrates: 29 g | Sugar: 6 g

Beer-Cheese Soup

For the best results, use a pale ale beer in this recipe.

INGREDIENTS | SERVES 12

½ cup butter or vegan margarine

½ white onion, diced

2 medium carrots, peeled and diced

2 ribs celery, diced

½ cup flour

3 cups Vegetable Broth (see recipe in this chapter)

1 (12-ounce) beer

3 cups milk or unsweetened soymilk

3 cups Cheddar cheese or vegan Daiya Cheddar style shreds

1 teaspoon salt

1 teaspoon pepper

½ teaspoon dry ground mustard

Unsweetened Soymilk

Plain or original soymilk typically contains sugar and has a distinct flavor that will stand out in savory dishes. For these recipes, use plain unsweetened soymilk instead.

1. In a sauté pan over medium heat, melt the butter or vegan margarine, then sauté the onion, carrots, and celery until just softened, about 5–7 minutes. Add the flour and stir to form a roux. Let cook for 2–3 minutes.

2. In a 4-quart slow cooker, add the cooked vegetables and roux, then slowly pour in the Vegetable Broth and beer while whisking.

3. Add the milk, cheese, salt, pepper, and mustard. Cover and cook on low for 4 hours.

4. Let the soup cool slightly, then blend until smooth, or you can skip this step and serve chunky.

PER SERVING Calories: 275 | Fat: 19 g | Protein: 10.5 g | Sodium: 462.5 mg | Fiber: 2 g | Carbohydrates: 14 g | Sugar: 6 g

Pumpkin-Ale Soup

Use fresh pumpkin in place of the canned pumpkin purée when the ingredient is in season.
You'll need 3¾ cup of cooked, pureed fresh pumpkin.

INGREDIENTS | SERVES 6

2 (15-ounce) cans pumpkin purée

¼ cup diced onion

2 cloves garlic, minced

2 teaspoons salt

1 teaspoon pepper

¼ teaspoon dried thyme

5 cups Vegetable Broth (see recipe in this chapter)

1 (12-ounce) bottle pale ale beer

1. In a 4-quart slow cooker, add the pumpkin purée, onion, garlic, salt, pepper, thyme, and Vegetable Broth. Stir well. Cover and cook over low heat for 4 hours.

2. Allow the soup to cool slightly, then process in a blender or with an immersion blender until smooth.

3. Pour the soup back into the slow cooker, add the beer, and cook for 1 hour over low heat.

PER SERVING Calories: 108 | Fat: 0 g | Protein: 3 g | Sodium: 854 mg | Fiber: 3 g | Carbohydrates: 22 g | Sugar: 7 g

Butternut Squash Soup

You can substitute an extra cup of vegetable broth for the white wine in this soup.

INGREDIENTS | SERVES 6

1 medium butternut squash, peeled and diced

1 russet potato, peeled and diced

1 large carrot, chopped

1 rib celery, sliced

1 onion, diced

4 cups Vegetable Broth (see recipe in this chapter)

1 cup white wine

1 bay leaf

¼ teaspoon dried thyme

1½ teaspoons salt

Pinch of nutmeg

1. In a 4-quart slow cooker, add all of the ingredients. Cover and cook over low heat for 6 hours.

2. Cool the soup slightly and remove the bay leaf. Process in a blender or using an immersion blender.

PER SERVING Calories: 115 | Fat: 0 g | Protein: 3 g | Sodium: 687 mg | Fiber: 4.5 g | Carbohydrates: 20 g | Sugar: 7 g

Vegetable Cuts

When chopping vegetables for a dish that will be blended, save time by not trying to make them too perfect or too small.

Tomato Basil Soup

Fresh basil adds a different flavor than dried basil to dishes,
and the fresh variety is more complementary to this soup.

INGREDIENTS | SERVES 5

2 tablespoons butter or vegan margarine
½ onion, diced
2 cloves garlic, minced
1 (28-ounce) can whole peeled tomatoes
½ cup Vegetable Broth (see recipe in this chapter)
1 bay leaf
1 teaspoon salt
1 teaspoon pepper
½ cup unsweetened soymilk
¼ cup sliced fresh basil

1. In a sauté pan over medium heat, melt the butter or margarine, then sauté the onion and garlic for 3–4 minutes.

2. In a 4-quart slow cooker, add the onion and garlic, tomatoes, Vegetable Broth, bay leaf, salt, and pepper. Cover and cook over low heat 4 hours.

3. Allow to cool slightly, then remove the bay leaf. Process the soup in a blender or immersion blender.

4. Return the soup to the slow cooker, then add the soymilk and chopped basil, and heat on low for an additional 30 minutes.

PER SERVING Calories: 95 | Fat: 5.5 g | Protein: 3 g | Sodium: 501 mg | Fiber: 3 g | Carbohydrates: 10.5 g | Sugar: 6 g

Creamy Chickpea Soup

Beans can be puréed to make a creamy soup without the cream.

INGREDIENTS | SERVES 6

1 small onion, diced

2 cloves garlic, minced

2 (15-ounce) cans chickpeas, drained and rinsed

5 cups Vegetable Broth (see recipe in this chapter)

1 teaspoon salt

½ teaspoon cumin

Juice of ½ lemon

1 tablespoon olive oil

¼ fresh parsley, chopped

1. In a 4-quart slow cooker, add all ingredients except for the lemon juice, olive oil, and parsley. Cover, and cook over low heat for 4 hours.

2. Allow to cool slightly, then process the soup in a blender or using an immersion blender.

3. Return the soup to the slow cooker, then add the lemon juice, olive oil, and parsley, and heat on low for an additional 30 minutes.

PER SERVING Calories: 205 | Fat: 11 g | Protein: 7 g | Sodium: 842 mg | Fiber: 6.5 g | Carbohydrates: 33 g | Sugar: 0.5 g

Minestrone Soup

Minestrone is a classic Italian vegetable soup.
The zucchini and cabbage are added at the end for a burst of fresh flavor.

INGREDIENTS | SERVES 8

3 cloves garlic, minced

1 (15-ounce) can fire-roasted diced tomatoes

1 (28-ounce) can crushed tomatoes

2 stalks celery, diced

1 medium onion, diced

3 medium carrots, diced

3 cups Vegetable Broth (see recipe in this chapter)

2 (15-ounce) cans kidney beans, drained and rinsed

2 tablespoons tomato paste

2 tablespoons minced basil

2 tablespoons minced oregano

2 tablespoons minced Italian parsley

1½ cups shredded cabbage

¾ cup diced zucchini

1 teaspoon salt

½ teaspoon pepper

8 ounces small cooked pasta

1. In a 4-quart slow cooker, add the garlic, diced and crushed tomatoes, celery, onions, carrots, broth, beans, tomato paste, basil, and spices. Cover and cook on low heat for 6–8 hours.

2. Add shredded cabbage and zucchini and turn to high for the last hour.

3. Stir in the salt, pepper, and pasta before serving.

PER SERVING Calories: 470 | Fat: 1.5 g | Protein: 28 g | Sodium: 320 mg | Fiber: 21 g | Carbohydrates: 89 g | Sugar: 11.5 g

Suggested Pasta Shapes for Soup

Anchellini, small shells, hoops, alfabeto, or ditaletti are all small pasta shapes suitable for soup. For heartier soups, try bow ties or rotini. Thin rice noodles or vermicelli are better for Asian-style soups.

Mushroom Barley Soup

Using three types of mushrooms in this soup adds a more robust flavor.

INGREDIENTS | SERVES 8

1 ounce dried porcini mushrooms

1 cup boiling water

1½ teaspoons butter or vegan margarine

5 ounces fresh shiitake mushrooms, sliced

4 ounces fresh button mushrooms, sliced

1 large onion, diced

1 clove garlic, minced

⅔ cup medium pearl barley

¼ teaspoon ground black pepper

½ teaspoon salt

6 cups No-Beef Broth (see recipe in this chapter)

1. In a heat-safe bowl, place the dried porcini mushrooms; pour the boiling water over the mushrooms. Soak for 15 minutes.

2. Meanwhile, in a medium sauté pan, melt the butter or vegan margarine. Sauté the fresh mushrooms, onion, and garlic until the onions are soft, about 3 minutes.

3. Drain the porcini mushrooms and discard the water.

4. In a 4-quart slow cooker, add all of the mushrooms, onions, garlic, barley, pepper, salt, and the broth. Stir, cover, and cook 6–8 hours on low.

PER SERVING Calories: 117 | Fat: 1 g | Protein: 4 g | Sodium: 210 mg | Fiber: 5.5 g | Carbohydrates: 24 g | Sugar: 6 g

Summer Borscht

Serve this cooling soup with a dollop of sour cream or vegan sour cream.
Try Tofutti's Sour Supreme.

INGREDIENTS | SERVES 6

3½ cups cooked beets, shredded

¼ cup onion, diced

½ teaspoon salt

1 teaspoon sugar

¼ cup lemon juice

½ tablespoon celery seed

2 cups Vegetable Broth (see recipe in this chapter)

2 cups water

1. In a 4-quart slow cooker, place all of the ingredients. Cover and cook on low for 6–8 hours, or on high for 4 hours.

2. Refrigerate the soup for 4 hours or overnight. Serve cold.

PER SERVING Calories: 60 | Fat: 0.5 g | Protein: 2 g | Sodium: 287.5 mg | Fiber: 4 g | Carbohydrates: 14 g | Sugar: 8 g

Can't Beat Beets

Beets, also known as beetroot, can be peeled, steamed, cooked, pickled, and shredded; they are good hot or cold. They are high in folate, vitamin C, potassium, and fiber. Although they have the highest sugar content of all vegetables, beets are very low in calories; one beet is only 75 calories.

Simple Split Pea Soup

Immersion blenders are hand-held blenders that can be used in the pot where food is cooked, which eliminates the need to transfer soup to a blender.

INGREDIENTS | SERVES 6

2 cups dried green split peas

Water, as needed

6 cups Vegetable Broth (see recipe in this chapter)

2 medium potatoes, peeled and diced

2 large carrots, chopped

3 stalks celery, chopped

2 cloves garlic, minced

1 teaspoon cumin

1 teaspoon thyme

1 bay leaf

1 teaspoon salt

1. Rinse the green split peas; soak overnight in enough water to cover them by more than 1". Drain.

2. In a 4-quart slow cooker, add all ingredients; cook over low heat for 6–8 hours.

3. Let the soup cool slightly, then remove the bay leaf. Process in a blender, or use an immersion blender, until smooth.

PER SERVING Calories: 155.5 | Fat: 0 g | Protein: 6 g | Sodium: 510 mg | Fiber: 8 g | Carbohydrates: 33.5 g | Sugar: 11 g

Tortilla Soup

Turn this soup into a complete meal by adding pieces of cooked vegetarian chicken, such as Morningstar Farms Meal Starters Chik'n Strips or Gardein Seasoned Bites.

INGREDIENTS | SERVES 8

2 tablespoons olive oil

1 large onion, chopped

2 cloves garlic, minced

2 tablespoons soy sauce

7 cups Vegetable Broth (see recipe in this chapter)

12 ounces firm silken tofu, crumbled

2 cups tomato, diced

1 cup corn kernels

1 teaspoon chipotle powder

1 teaspoon cayenne pepper

2 teaspoons ground cumin

2 teaspoons salt

1 teaspoon dried oregano

10 small corn tortillas, sliced

8 ounces shredded Monterey Jack cheese or vegan cheese, such as Daiya Mozzarella Style Shreds

Chipotle Powder

Chipotle powder is made from ground chipotle peppers, a type of dried jalapeño. They bring a smoky spiciness to dishes, but can be replaced with cayenne pepper or chili powder.

1. In a sauté pan over medium heat, add the olive oil; sauté the onions until just soft, about 3 minutes. Add the garlic and sauté for an additional 30 seconds.

2. In a 4-quart slow cooker, add all ingredients except tortillas and cheese. Stir, cover, and cook over low heat for 4 hours.

3. While the soup is cooking, Preheat oven to 450°F. Slice the corn tortillas into thin strips and place them on an ungreased baking sheet. Bake for about 10 minutes, or until they turn golden brown. Remove from heat and set aside.

4. After the soup has cooled slightly, use an immersion blender or regular blender to purée the soup.

5. Serve with cooked tortilla strips and 1 ounce of shredded cheese in each bowl of soup.

PER SERVING Calories: 298 | Fat: 15 g | Protein: 14 g | Sodium: 1,043 mg | Fiber: 4.5 g | Carbohydrates: 29 g | Sugar: 5 g

Greek-Style Orzo and Spinach Soup

Lemon zest adds a bright, robust flavor to this simple soup.

INGREDIENTS | SERVES 6

2 cloves garlic, minced

3 tablespoons lemon juice

1 teaspoon lemon zest

5 cups Vegetable Broth (see recipe in this chapter

1½ teaspoons salt

1 small onion, thinly sliced

1 package extra-firm tofu, cubed

⅓ cup dried orzo

4 cups fresh baby spinach

1. In a 4-quart slow cooker, add the garlic, lemon juice, zest, broth, salt, and onion. Cover and cook on low for 6–8 hours.

2. Stir in the tofu and cook for 30 minutes on high.

3. Add the orzo and spinach. Stir and continue to cook on high for an additional 15 minutes. Stir before serving.

PER SERVING Calories: 87 | Fat: 3 g | Protein: 9 g | Sodium: 647 mg | Fiber: 1 g | Carbohydrates: 7 g | Sugar: 2 g

Quick Tip: Zesting

There are many tools on the market that are for zesting citrus, but all you really need is a fine grater. Be sure to take off the outermost part of the peel, where the aromatic essential oils that hold the flavor are located. The white pith underneath is bitter and inedible.

Pho

This Vietnamese noodle soup is easy to make in the slow cooker.
Try it instead of vegetable soup on a cold night.

INGREDIENTS | SERVES 6

1 tablespoon coriander seeds

1 tablespoon whole cloves

6 star anise

1 cinnamon stick

1 tablespoon fennel seed

1 tablespoon whole cardamom

4 knobs fresh ginger, sliced

1 onion, sliced

1 quart No-Beef Broth (see recipe in this chapter)

1 teaspoon soy sauce

8 ounces Vietnamese rice noodles

1 cup shredded seitan

½ cup chopped cilantro

½ cup chopped Thai basil

2 cups mung bean sprouts

¼ cup sliced scallions

1. In a dry nonstick skillet, quickly heat the spices, ginger, and onion until the seeds start to pop, about 5 minutes. The onion and ginger should look slightly caramelized. Place them in a cheesecloth packet and tie it securely.

2. In a 4-quart slow cooker, place the cheesecloth packet. Add the broth, soy sauce, noodles, and seitan. Cover and cook on low for 4 hours.

3. Remove the cheesecloth packet after cooking. Serve each bowl topped with cilantro, basil, sprouts, and scallions.

PER SERVING Calories: 267 | Fat: 12 g | Protein: 7 g | Sodium: 272 mg | Fiber: 5 g | Carbohydrates: 36 g | Sugar: 5 g

Wild Rice and Portobello Soup

Any variety of rice will work in this soup. It's fine to substitute white rice or brown rice if that's all you have on hand.

INGREDIENTS | SERVES 4

½ yellow onion, diced

2 small carrots, peeled and diced

2 ribs celery, sliced

1 cup chopped Portobello mushroom

½ cup uncooked wild rice

4 cups Vegetable Broth (see recipe in this chapter)

1 bay leaf

1 sprig rosemary

1 teaspoon salt

½ teaspoon pepper

1. In a 4-quart slow cooker, add all ingredients. Cover and cook over low heat for 6 hours.

2. Remove the bay leaf and rosemary sprig before serving.

PER SERVING Calories: 167 | Fat: 0.5 g | Protein: 6 g | Sodium: 791 mg | Fiber: 8 g | Carbohydrates: 36 g | Sugar: 11 g

Celery Root Soup

Serve a bowl of this soup topped with green apple crisps.

INGREDIENTS | SERVES 6

2 tablespoons butter or vegan margarine

1 small leek (white and light green parts only), chopped

2 cloves garlic, minced

1 large celery root, peeled and cubed

2 medium russet potatoes, peeled and cubed

6 cups Vegetable Broth (see recipe in this chapter)

1½ teaspoons salt

1 teaspoon pepper

Celery Root

Celery root, also known as celeriac, is not the root of the celery you know. It is similar in texture to a potato, and is cultivated for its root, not its leaves or stalk. It is grown in cool weather and is best in the fall, right after it has been pulled. The roots and crevices have to be trimmed away, so a 1-pound root will only yield about 2 cups after it is peeled and sliced or grated, something to keep in mind when buying for a recipe.

1. In a large sauté pan over medium heat, melt the butter or margarine, then add the leeks and sauté about 4 minutes. Add the garlic and sauté an additional 30 seconds.

2. In a 4-quart slow cooker, add the sautéed leeks and garlic, celery root, potatoes, broth, salt, and pepper. Cover and cook over low heat for 6–8 hours.

3. Let the soup cool slightly, then process in a blender or with an immersion blender until smooth.

PER SERVING Calories: 147.5 | Fat: 4 g | Protein: 3 g | Sodium: 679 mg | Fiber: 5 g | Carbohydrates: 26 g | Sugar: 7 g

CHAPTER 4

Stews

Brunswick Stew

Try adding barbecue sauce to this stew to spice things up.

INGREDIENTS | SERVES 4

4 cups Vegetable Broth (see Chapter 3)
1 (15-ounce) can diced tomatoes
1 (6-ounce) can tomato paste
1 cup okra, sliced
1 cup corn
1 cup frozen lima beans
2 cups seitan, diced
¼ teaspoon dried rosemary
¼ teaspoon dried oregano
2 teaspoons vegan Worcestershire sauce
Salt and pepper, to taste

In a 4-quart slow cooker, add all ingredients. Cover and cook on low heat for 5–6 hours.

PER SERVING Calories: 273 | Fat: 6 g | Protein: 15 g | Sodium: 702 mg | Fiber: 7 g | Carbohydrates: 44 g | Sugar: 10 g

Debate on Origin

Some claim that Brunswick stew was first served in Brunswick, Georgia, in 1898, while others say it was created in Brunswick County, Virginia, in 1828. Today, Brunswick Stew recipe ingredients vary by region.

Jamaican Red Bean Stew

Make your own jerk seasoning by combining thyme, allspice, black pepper, cinnamon, cayenne, onion powder, and nutmeg.

INGREDIENTS | SERVES 4

2 tablespoons olive oil

½ onion, diced

2 garlic cloves, minced

1 (15-ounce) can diced tomatoes

3 cups sweet potatoes, peeled and diced

2 (15-ounce) cans red kidney beans, drained

1 cup coconut milk

3 cups Vegetable Broth (see Chapter 3)

2 teaspoons jerk seasoning

2 teaspoons curry powder

Salt and pepper, to taste

1. In a sauté pan over medium heat, add the olive oil, then sauté the onion and garlic for about 3 minutes.

2. In a 4-quart slow cooker, add all ingredients. Cover and cook on low heat for 6 hours.

PER SERVING Calories: 493 | Fat: 19 g | Protein: 15 g | Sodium: 755 mg | Fiber: 15 g | Carbohydrates: 60 g | Sugar: 11 g

Southwest Corn Chowder

The russet potatoes in this recipe will slowly break up during the cooking process and add to the creaminess of the chowder.

INGREDIENTS | SERVES 4

¼ cup butter or vegan margarine

1 onion, diced

1 jalapeño, minced

1 cup diced tomato

2 medium russet potatoes, peeled and diced

2 (15-ounce) cans creamed corn

2 cups water

2 cups unsweetened soymilk

1 teaspoon chili powder

1 teaspoon cumin

¼ teaspoon cayenne pepper

Salt and pepper, to taste

1. In a sauté pan over medium heat, melt the butter or vegan margarine; add the onion and jalapeño, and sauté for about 3 minutes.

2. In a 4-quart slow cooker, add all ingredients. Cover and cook on low heat for 6 hours.

PER SERVING Calories: 437 | Fat: 16 g | Protein: 12 g | Sodium: 846 mg | Fiber: 9 g | Carbohydrates: 69 g | Sugar: 14 g

Creamed Corn

Some creamed corn recipes don't get their creaminess from dairy products; it's from the milky substance that comes from the cob after the kernels are removed.

Okra Gumbo

The roux—a combination of oil or butter and flour—is the base for many classic New Orleans dishes.

INGREDIENTS | SERVES 6

½ cup vegetable oil

½ cup flour

1 white onion, diced

1 bell pepper, diced

4 cloves garlic, minced

4 cups water

2 cups Vegetable Broth (see Chapter 3)

1 tablespoon vegan Worcestershire sauce

1 (16-ounce) package frozen chopped okra

1 tablespoon Cajun seasoning

1 bay leaf

2 teaspoons salt

2 teaspoons pepper

1 (7-ounce) package Gardein Chick'n Strips, chopped

½ cup flat-leaf parsley, chopped

½ cup scallions, sliced

½ teaspoon file powder

6 cups cooked white rice

1. In a sauté pan, bring the oil and flour to medium heat, stirring continuously until the roux achieves a rich brown color, at least 10 minutes.

2. In a 4-quart slow cooker, add the roux and all remaining ingredients except the rice. Cover and cook on low heat for 6 hours.

3. Once done, remove the bay leaf. Pour each serving over 1 cup of cooked rice.

PER SERVING Calories: 523 | Fat: 19 g | Protein: 10 g | Sodium: 910 mg | Fiber: 5 g | Carbohydrates: 76.5 g | Sugar: 6 g

File Powder

File (pronounced FEE-lay) powder is made from ground sassafras leaves. It is an essential ingredient for authentic Cajun or Creole gumbo. Used to both thicken and flavor, file powder is thought to have been first used by the Choctaw Indians from the Louisiana bayou region. It can be found in most well-stocked grocery stores.

Mediterranean Vegetable Stew

Try serving this stew with large pieces of pita bread and a scoop of hummus.

INGREDIENTS | SERVES 6

2 tablespoons extra-virgin olive oil

4 garlic cloves, chopped

1 red onion, chopped

1 red bell pepper, seeded and chopped

1 eggplant, chopped

1 (15-ounce) can artichokes, drained and chopped

⅓ cup kalamata olives, pitted and chopped

2 (15-ounce) cans diced tomatoes

4 cups Vegetable Broth (see Chapter 3)

1 teaspoon red pepper flakes

½ teaspoon dried oregano

½ teaspoon dried parsley

1 teaspoon salt

½ teaspoon pepper

In a 4-quart slow cooker, add all ingredients. Cover and cook on low heat for 4–6 hours.

PER SERVING Calories: 214 | Fat: 6 g | Protein: 6 g | Sodium: 522 mg | Fiber: 8 g | Carbohydrates: 31 g | Sugar: 12 g

Preparing Eggplant

Some people salt eggplant prior to cooking in order to remove bitterness, but this step is not required for making delicious recipes using eggplant. The skins can be removed, but this also is not necessary. Eggplants, called aubergine in almost all other parts of the world, can be boiled, steamed, sautéed, stir-fried, deep-fried, braised, baked, grilled, broiled, and microwaved.

White Bean and Tomato Stew

Enjoy this hearty stew over rice or with a piece of crusty white bread.

INGREDIENTS | SERVES 4

1 (15-ounce) can cannellini beans, drained

4 cups Vegetable Broth (see Chapter 3)

1 tablespoon vegetable oil

1 teaspoon salt

2 cloves garlic, minced

½ teaspoon dried sage

¼ teaspoon dried thyme

½ teaspoon black pepper

1 cup tomato, diced

1. In a 4-quart slow cooker, add all ingredients except for tomato. Cover and cook on low heat for 5–6 hours.

2. Add the tomato; stir, and cook for an additional 30 minutes.

PER SERVING Calories: 128 | Fat: 4 g | Protein: 6 g | Sodium: 809 mg | Fiber: 6 g | Carbohydrates: 20 g | Sugar: 3 g

White Beans

Beans are an easy and delicious way to provide protein to a vegetarian or vegan diet. They are also low in fat and a good source of fiber. Cannellini, great northern, and navy are all types of white beans. Each has its own unique flavor. Cannellini are the largest, and have an earthy flavor.

Seitan and Mushroom Stew

*Homemade or store-bought seitan will work well in this recipe,
but if you use store bought, be sure to drain the liquid first.*

INGREDIENTS | SERVES 4

2 tablespoons extra-virgin olive oil

1 yellow onion, sliced

4 garlic cloves, minced

1 cup carrots, chopped

2 cups mushrooms, sliced

2 cups seitan, cubed

3 cups Vegetable Broth (see Chapter 3)

2 tablespoons soy sauce

1 cup potatoes, peeled and cubed

1 cup frozen peas

½ teaspoon sage

½ teaspoon salt

¼ teaspoon pepper

1. In a sauté pan over medium heat, add the extra virgin olive oil. Add the onions and garlic and sauté for 3 minutes.

2. In a 4-quart slow cooker, add the sautéed vegetables and all remaining ingredients. Cover and cook on low heat for 4–5 hours.

PER SERVING Calories: 207 | Fat: 7 g | Protein: 9 g | Sodium: 891 mg | Fiber: 9.5 g | Carbohydrates: 28.5 g | Sugar: 10 g

Curried Seitan Stew

Adding a small amount of soy sauce to a curry dish gives it a richness that is normally achieved with fish sauce in recipes that aren't vegetarian.

INGREDIENTS | SERVES 4

2 tablespoons olive oil

½ onion, chopped

2 cloves garlic, minced

1 teaspoon fresh ginger, minced

2 tablespoons Panang curry paste

1 teaspoon paprika

1 teaspoon sugar

½ teaspoon cayenne pepper

1 teaspoon soy sauce

1 (14-ounce) can coconut milk

3 cups Vegetable Broth (see Chapter 3)

2 cups seitan, cubed

½ teaspoon salt

¼ teaspoon pepper

¼ cup cilantro, chopped

1. In a 4-quart slow cooker, add all ingredients except for the cilantro. Cover and cook on low heat for 4 hours.

2. Garnish with cilantro before serving.

PER SERVING Calories: 322 | Fat: 28 g | Protein: 6.5 g | Sodium: 209 mg | Fiber: 6 g | Carbohydrates: 16 g | Sugar: 6 g

Vegetable Dumpling Stew

Surprisingly, some popular brands of uncooked biscuits in a tube are actually vegan.

INGREDIENTS | SERVES 6

2 tablespoons olive oil

½ large onion, diced

2 cloves garlic, minced

2 carrots, chopped

2 stalks celery, chopped

½ cup corn kernels

½ cup okra, chopped

2 (14½-ounce) cans diced tomatoes

4 cups Vegetable Broth (see Chapter 3)

¼ teaspoon dried rosemary

1 teaspoon dried parsley

¼ teaspoon dried oregano

½ teaspoon salt

¼ teaspoon black pepper

1 (6-ounce) package vegan refrigerated biscuits

1. In a sauté pan over medium heat, add the olive oil, onion, and garlic and sauté for 3 minutes.

2. In a 4-quart slow cooker, add all ingredients except for the biscuits, Cover and cook on low heat for 4–5 hours.

3. While the stew is cooking, flatten the biscuits with a rolling pin on a floured surface, then cut each into fourths.

4. Drop the biscuit pieces into the stew and cook for 30 more minutes.

PER SERVING Calories: 215 | Fat: 7 g | Protein: 6 g | Sodium: 433 mg | Fiber: 6 g | Carbohydrates: 35 g | Sugar: 11 g

Étouffée

Vegan shrimp can be purchased online at CosmosVeganShoppe.com.

INGREDIENTS | SERVES 6

½ cup butter or vegan margarine

1 onion, diced

3 celery ribs, chopped

1 carrot, diced

3 cloves garlic, minced

1 green bell pepper, chopped

¼ cup flour

1 cup water

2 teaspoons Cajun seasoning

1 (10.5-ounce) package vegan shrimp

Juice of 1 lemon

½ teaspoon salt

¼ teaspoon black pepper

4 cups cooked white rice

½ cup parsley, chopped

Cajun Seasoning

To make your own Cajun seasoning, use a blend of equal parts cayenne pepper, black pepper, paprika, garlic powder, onion powder, salt, and thyme.

1. In a sauté pan over medium heat, add the butter or vegan margarine. Sauté the onion, celery, carrot, garlic, and green bell pepper until soft, about 5–7 minutes. Stir in the flour to make a roux.

2. Add the roux to a 4-quart slow cooker. Whisk in the water, Cajun seasoning, vegan shrimp, lemon juice, salt, and pepper. Cover and cook on low heat for 4–5 hours.

3. Serve over the white rice and garnish with parsley.

PER SERVING Calories: 410 | Fat: 167 g | Protein: 15 g | Sodium: 381 mg | Fiber: 4 g | Carbohydrates: 49 g | Sugar: 4 g

Seitan and Cabbage Stew

This dish is reminiscent of beef and cabbage stew, minus the meat.

INGREDIENTS | SERVES 4

1 onion, chopped

1 carrot, chopped

2 celery ribs, chopped

4 cups cabbage, shredded

2 potatoes, chopped

3 cups seitan, cubed

4 cups Vegetable Broth (see Chapter 3)

2 tablespoons vegan Worcestershire sauce

½ teaspoon salt

¼ teaspoon black pepper

In a 4-quart slow cooker, add all ingredients. Cover and cook on low heat for 5–6 hours.

PER SERVING Calories: 232 | Fat: 1 g | Protein: 13 g | Sodium: 678 mg | Fiber: 6 g | Carbohydrates: 28 g | Sugar: 6 g

Posole

This rich-tasting stew just needs a sprinkling of shredded red cabbage to finish it to perfection.

INGREDIENTS | SERVES 6

8 large dried New Mexican red chiles

1½ quarts Vegetable Broth (see Chapter 3)

3 cloves garlic, minced

2 tablespoons lime juice

1 tablespoon ground cumin

1 tablespoon oregano

1 (7-ounce) package Gardein Chick'n Strips

¾ cup flour

1 teaspoon canola oil

1 large onion, sliced

40 ounces canned hominy

Citrus Leftovers

If you have a small amount of juice left, pour it into an ice cube tray in your freezer, one well at a time, and freeze. Leftover zest can also be saved. Place the zest in a freezer bag and refrigerate up to 1 week or frozen in a freezer-safe container up to 1 month.

1. Seed the chiles, reserving the seeds.

2. In a dry, hot frying pan, heat the chiles until warmed through and fragrant, about 2–3 minutes. Do not burn or brown them.

3. In a medium pot, place the chiles and seeds, 1 quart broth, garlic, lime juice, cumin, and oregano. Bring to a boil and continue to boil for 20 minutes.

4. Meanwhile, in a plastic bag, toss the chick'n strips with the flour to coat. Heat the oil in a large nonstick skillet and brown the vegan meat on all sides, about 3 minutes.

5. Add the onions and cook about 5 minutes, or until the onions are soft.

6. In a 4-quart slow cooker, pour the unused broth, hominy, the onion, and chick'n mixture.

7. Strain the chile-stock mixture through a mesh sieve into the slow cooker insert, mashing down with a wooden spoon to press out the pulp and juice. Discard the seeds and remaining solids.

8. Cook on low for 8 hours.

PER SERVING Calories: 824 | Fat: 4 g | Protein: 22.5 g | Sodium: 147.5 mg | Fiber: 11 g | Carbohydrates: 182 g | Sugar: 12 g

Pumpkin Stew

In chunky stews, fresh pumpkin works best, but if you are going to purée it into a creamy soup, then canned pumpkin is the better choice.

INGREDIENTS | SERVES 8

6 cups Vegetable Broth (see Chapter 3)

2 cups pumpkin, cubed and peeled

2 cups potatoes, cubed and peeled

1 cup corn kernels

1 onion, diced

2 cloves garlic, minced

2 bay leaves

2 tablespoons tomato paste

1½ teaspoons salt

½ teaspoon dried thyme

½ teaspoon dried parsley

In a 4-quart slow cooker, add all ingredients. Cover and cook over low heat for 8 hours.

PER SERVING Calories: 102 | Fat: 0 g | Protein: 3 g | Sodium: 536.5 mg | Fiber: 4 g | Carbohydrates: 24 g | Sugar: 7 g

Cauliflower Chowder

In this rich chowder, puréed cauliflower takes the place of heavy cream or soymilk.

INGREDIENTS | SERVES 6

2 pounds cauliflower florets

2 quarts Vegetable Broth (see Chapter 3)

1 onion, chopped

3 cloves garlic, minced

1 teaspoon white pepper

1½ teaspoons salt

1½ cups broccoli florets

2 carrots, cut into coins

1 stalk celery, diced

1. In a 4-quart slow cooker, place the cauliflower, broth, onions, garlic, pepper, and salt; stir. Cook on low for 6 hours, or until the cauliflower is fork tender.

2. Use an immersion blender to purée the cauliflower in the slow cooker until very smooth.

3. Add the broccoli, carrots, and celery. Cook for 30 minutes, or until the vegetables are fork-tender.

PER SERVING Calories: 135 | Fat: 0.5 g | Protein: 6 g | Sodium: 767 mg | Fiber: 9 g | Carbohydrates: 30 g | Sugar: 13 g

White Bean Cassoulet

The longer you cook this cassoulet, the creamier it gets.

INGREDIENTS | SERVES 8

1 pound dried cannellini beans
2 cups boiling water
1 ounce dried porcini mushrooms
2 leeks, sliced
1 teaspoon canola oil
2 parsnips, diced
2 carrots, diced
2 stalks celery, diced
½ teaspoon ground fennel
1 teaspoon crushed rosemary
1 teaspoon dried chervil
⅛ teaspoon cloves
¼ teaspoon salt
¼ teaspoon freshly ground black pepper
2 cups Vegetable Broth (see Chapter 3)

Using Dried Beans

Dried beans must be soaked overnight and boiled for at least 10 minutes before being added to a slow cooker, if you'd prefer to use them over canned beans.

1. The night before making the soup, place the beans in a 4-quart slow cooker. Fill with water to 1" below the top of the insert. Soak overnight.

2. Drain the beans and return them to the slow cooker.

3. In a heat-proof bowl, pour the boiling water over the dried mushrooms and soak for 15 minutes.

4. Slice only the white and light green parts of the leek into ¼ rounds. Cut the rounds in half.

5. In a nonstick skillet, heat the oil; add the parsnip, carrots, celery, and leeks. Sauté for 1 minute, just until the color of the vegetables brightens.

6. Add to the slow cooker along with the spices. Add the mushrooms, their soaking liquid, and the broth; stir.

7. Cook on low for 8–10 hours.

PER SERVING Calories: 220 | Fat: 1.5 g | Protein: 15 g | Sodium: 170 mg | Fiber: 10 g | Carbohydrates: 39 g | Sugar: 6 g

Korean-Style Hot Pot

Serve this hot and spicy main dish with sides of steamed rice and kimchi.

INGREDIENTS | SERVES 8

3 bunches baby bok choy

8 cups water

8 ounces sliced crimini mushrooms

12 ounces extra-firm tofu, cubed

3 cloves garlic, thinly sliced

¼ teaspoon sesame oil

1 tablespoon crushed red pepper flakes

7 ounces enoki mushrooms

1. Remove the leaves of the baby bok choy. Wash thoroughly.

2. Place the leaves whole in a 4-quart slow cooker. Add the water, crimini mushrooms, tofu, garlic, sesame oil, and crushed red pepper. Stir.

3. Cook on low for 8 hours.

4. Add the enoki mushrooms and stir. Cook an additional 30 minutes.

PER SERVING Calories: 80 | Fat: 2 g | Protein: 9 g | Sodium: 230 mg | Fiber: 4 g | Carbohydrates: 11 g | Sugar: 3 g

Seitan Bourguinon

Better Than Bouillon's No Beef Base is a good vegetarian alternative to beef stock.

INGREDIENTS | SERVES 6

2 tablespoons olive oil

1 pound cooked seitan, cut into 2" cubes

2 carrots, sliced

1 onion, sliced

1 teaspoon salt

2 tablespoons flour

2 cups red wine

2 cups No-Beef Broth (see Chapter 3)

1 tablespoon tomato paste

2 cloves garlic, minced

½ teaspoon dried thyme

1 bay leaf

¼ teaspoon pepper

1 tablespoon butter or vegan margarine

18 whole pearl onions, peeled

2 cups button mushrooms, sliced

1. Heat the olive oil in a sauté pan over medium heat. Sauté the seitan, carrots, and onion until soft, about 7 minutes. Stir in the salt and flour.

2. In a 4-quart slow cooker, add the vegetables and roux. Whisk in the red wine and No-Beef Broth, then add all remaining ingredients.

3. Cover and cook over low heat for 6–8 hours.

PER SERVING Calories: 280 | Fat: 8 g | Protein: 20 g | Sodium: 805 mg | Fiber: 3 g | Carbohydrates: 15 g | Sugar: 3.5 g

Seitan

Seitan is made from wheat gluten and is often used as a vegetarian substitute for all types of meat. It's one of the easiest meat substitutes to cook with at home; see Chapter 12 for more recipes.

Super Greens Stew

*Kale and Swiss chard can hold up during long cooking times,
but a more delicate green, such as spinach, would break down more.*

INGREDIENTS | SERVES 6

2 cups chopped kale

2 cups chopped Swiss chard

1 (15-ounce) can chickpeas, drained

¼ onion, diced

1 carrot, peeled and sliced

2 cloves garlic, minced

6 cups Vegetable Broth (see Chapter 3)

1½ teaspoons salt

½ teaspoon pepper

1 sprig rosemary

½ teaspoon dried marjoram

In a 4-quart slow cooker, add all ingredients. Cover, and cook on low heat for 6 hours.

PER SERVING Calories: 128 | Fat: 1.4 g | Protein: 6 g | Sodium: 727 mg | Fiber: 5 g | Carbohydrates: 20 g | Sugar: 2 g

Texas Stew

Simple yet hearty is the goal for this cowboy-style stew.

INGREDIENTS | SERVES 6

2 tablespoons olive oil

1 (12-ounce) package frozen veggie crumbles

1 (15-ounce) can pinto beans, drained

1 (14-ounce) can diced tomatoes

1 (12-ounce) package frozen corn

½ onion, diced

½ green bell pepper, diced

4 cups Vegetable Broth (see Chapter 3)

1 teaspoon salt

1. In a sauté pan over medium, heat the olive oil and cook the frozen veggie crumbles until browned, about 10 minutes.

2. In a 4-quart slow cooker, add the cooked veggie crumbles and all other ingredients. Cover, and cook on low heat for 4–6 hours.

PER SERVING Calories: 236 | Fat: 6 g | Protein: 9 g | Sodium: 772 mg | Fiber: 5 g | Carbohydrates: 42 g | Sugar: 6 g

Mock Meatball Stew

Unlike a traditional pasta dish, this stew has more sauce and just a little bit of pasta.

INGREDIENTS | SERVES 4

1 tablespoon olive oil

¼ onion, diced

3 cloves garlic, minced

1 teaspoon dried oregano

1 teaspoon dried basil

½ teaspoon crushed red pepper

1 teaspoon salt

2 cups Vegetable Broth (see Chapter 3)

2 (15-ounce) cans diced tomatoes

12 small vegan meatballs

2 cups cooked pasta shells

1. In a sauté pan over medium, heat the olive oil. Add the onion and sauté for 2–3 minutes.

2. Add the garlic and sauté for an additional 30 seconds.

3. In a 4-quart slow cooker, add the sautéed onion and garlic and all other ingredients except for the pasta. Cover and cook on low for 4–6 hours.

4. Add the pasta and cook 1 additional hour.

PER SERVING Calories: 285 | Fat: 8 g | Protein: 7 g | Sodium: 1,219 mg | Fiber: 7 g | Carbohydrates: 45 g | Sugar: 9 g

Vegan Meatballs

Meatless Meatballs by Nate's are delicious premade vegan meatballs that can be ordered from CosmosVeganShoppe.com or purchased in many major grocery stores.

CHAPTER 5

Chili

Southwest Vegetable Chili

Southwest cuisine is similar to Mexican food and includes a wide variety of peppers, such as the jalapeños, bell peppers, chipotle, and chili powder found in this recipe.

INGREDIENTS | SERVES 4

1 (28-ounce) can diced tomatoes
1 (15-ounce) can red kidney beans
1 onion, chopped
1 green bell pepper, chopped
1 red bell pepper, chopped
1 zucchini, chopped
1 squash, chopped
¼ cup pickled jalapeños, chopped
⅛ cup chili powder
2 tablespoons garlic powder
2 tablespoons cumin
1 teaspoon chipotle powder
⅛ teaspoon dried thyme
1 teaspoon salt
¼ teaspoon black pepper

In a 4-quart slow cooker, add all ingredients. Cover and cook on low heat for 5 hours.

PER SERVING Calories: 183 | Fat: 2 g | Protein: 10 g | Sodium: 675 mg | Fiber: 10 g | Carbohydrates: 33 g | Sugar: 12 g

Cincinnati Chili

Cincinnati chili is native to the state of Ohio and is typically eaten over spaghetti or on hot dogs.

INGREDIENTS | SERVES 4

1 onion, chopped

1 (12-ounce) package frozen veggie burger crumbles

3 cloves garlic, minced

1 cup tomato sauce

1 cup water

2 tablespoons red wine vinegar

2 tablespoons chili powder

½ teaspoon cumin

½ teaspoon ground cinnamon

½ teaspoon paprika

½ teaspoon ground allspice

1 tablespoon light brown sugar

1 tablespoon unsweetened cocoa powder

1 teaspoon hot pepper sauce

16 ounces cooked spaghetti

1. In a 4-quart slow cooker, add all ingredients except for the spaghetti and optional ingredients. Cover and cook on low heat for 5 hours.

2. Serve the chili over the spaghetti and top with cheese, onions, and/or pinto beans.

PER SERVING Calories: 329 | Fat: 6 g | Protein: 24.5 g | Sodium: 783 mg | Fiber: 2 g | Carbohydrates: 50 g | Sugar: 8 g

Ways to Serve

Cincinnati chili is known for being served up to five ways: Two-way means chili and spaghetti; three-way means chili, spaghetti, and cheddar cheese; four-way means chili, spaghetti, cheese, and onions or pinto beans; and five-way means all of the above!

Chili con "Carne"

Try Boca Ground Crumbles in this fast recipe as a vegan alternative to ground beef.

INGREDIENTS | SERVES 4

½ cup onion, diced

½ cup bell pepper, diced

1 (12-ounce) package frozen veggie burger crumbles

2 cloves garlic, minced

1 (15-ounce) can kidney beans, rinsed and drained

2 cups Vegetable Broth (see Chapter 3)

1 tablespoon chili powder

½ tablespoon chipotle powder

½ tablespoon cumin

1 teaspoon thyme

1 tablespoon oregano

2 cups fresh tomatoes, diced

1 tablespoon tomato paste

1 tablespoon cider vinegar

2 teaspoons salt

In a 4-quart slow cooker, add all ingredients. Cover and cook on low heat for 5 hours.

PER SERVING Calories: 249 | Fat: 3 g | Protein: 12 g | Sodium: 1,685.5 mg | Fiber: 8 g | Carbohydrates: 36 g | Sugar: 7 g

Vegan Beef

In addition to Boca Ground Crumbles, there are other types of vegetarian ground beef on the market. Try Gimme Lean Ground Beef Style or Morningstar Farms Crumbles (not suitable for vegans) for a prepackaged option. Or try using dehydrated textures vegetable protein (TVP).

Shredded "Chicken" Chili

There are many vegan and vegetarian chicken substitutes on the market,
but you can also use shredded seitan to replace the meat.

INGREDIENTS | SERVES 4

½ cup onion, diced

½ cup bell pepper, diced

1 (8-ounce) package Morningstar Farms Meal Starter Chik'n Strips, shredded by hand

2 cloves garlic, minced

1 (15-ounce) can kidney beans, rinsed and drained

2 cups Vegetable Broth (see Chapter 3)

1 tablespoon chili powder

½ tablespoon chipotle powder

½ tablespoon cumin

1 teaspoon thyme

1 tablespoon oregano

1 (15-ounce) can diced tomatoes, drained

1 tablespoon tomato paste

1 tablespoon cider vinegar

2 teaspoons salt

In a 4-quart slow cooker, add all ingredients. Cover and cook on low heat for 5 hours.

PER SERVING Calories: 303 | Fat: 5 g | Protein: 20 g | Sodium: 1,582 mg | Fiber: 7 g | Carbohydrates: 20 g | Sugar: 3 g

Five-Pepper Chili

Sound the alarm! This chili will set mouths aflame.

INGREDIENTS | SERVES 8

1 onion, diced

1 jalapeño, seeded and minced

1 habanero pepper, seeded and minced

1 bell pepper, diced

1 poblano pepper, seeded and diced

2 cloves garlic, minced

2 (15-ounce) cans crushed tomatoes

2 cups fresh tomatoes, diced

2 tablespoons chili powder

1 tablespoon cumin

½ tablespoon cayenne pepper

⅛ cup vegan Worcestershire sauce

2 (15-ounce) cans pinto beans

1 teaspoon salt

¼ teaspoon black pepper

In a 4-quart slow cooker, add all ingredients. Cover and cook on low heat for 5 hours.

PER SERVING Calories: 142 | Fat: 2 g | Protein: 7 g | Sodium: 820 mg | Fiber: 8 g | Carbohydrates: 27 g | Sugar: 6 g

Sweet Potato Chili

Sweet potatoes are great sources of fiber and beta carotene, making this chili healthy and delicious.

INGREDIENTS | SERVES 4

1 red onion, diced

1 jalapeño, seeded and minced

3 cloves garlic, minced

1 (15-ounce) can black beans, drained

1 sweet potato, peeled and diced

3 tablespoons chili powder

1 tablespoon paprika

1 teaspoon dried oregano

1 teaspoon ground cumin

½ teaspoon chipotle powder

1 (28-ounce) can diced tomatoes, drained

2 cups Vegetable Broth (see Chapter 3)

1 teaspoon salt

¼ teaspoon black pepper

1 lime, juiced

¼ cup cilantro, chopped

1. In a 4-quart slow cooker, add all ingredients except the lime and cilantro. Cover and cook on low heat for 8 hours.

2. When the chili is done cooking, mix in the lime juice and garnish with the cilantro.

PER SERVING Calories: 220 | Fat: 2 g | Protein: 10 g | Sodium: 1,297 mg | Fiber: 8 g | Carbohydrates: 45 g | Sugar: 13 g

What Is Chili Powder?

Chili powder is made from grinding dried chilis, and may be created from a blend of different types of chilis or just one variety. The most commonly used chilis are red peppers and cayenne peppers.

Three-Bean Chili

Using dried beans will save you a little money on this recipe, but be sure to soak the beans overnight and boil for 10 minutes on the stove top before using.

INGREDIENTS | SERVES 8

1 (15-ounce) can pinto beans, drained

1 (15-ounce) can black beans, drained

1 (15-ounce) can great northern white beans, drained

1 onion, diced

3 cloves garlic, minced

3 cups Vegetable Broth (see Chapter 3)

1 tablespoon chili powder

½ tablespoon chipotle powder

½ tablespoon cumin

½ tablespoon paprika

1 (15-ounce) can diced tomatoes

1 teaspoon salt

¼ teaspoon black pepper

In a 4-quart slow cooker, add all ingredients. Cover and cook on low heat for 5 hours.

PER SERVING Calories: 174 | Fat: 2 g | Protein: 10 g | Sodium: 727 mg | Fiber: 9 g | Carbohydrates: 37 g | Sugar: 4 g

Fajita Chili

Recreate the flavor of sizzling restaurant fajitas in your own home!

INGREDIENTS | SERVES 6

1 red onion, diced

1 jalapeño, seeded and minced

3 cloves garlic, minced

1 (15-ounce) can black beans, drained

1 (15-ounce) can diced tomatoes, drained

1 (8-ounce) package Morningstar Farms Meal Starter Chik'n Strips, cut into bite-size pieces

2 cups Vegetable Broth (see Chapter 3)

2 teaspoons chili powder

1 teaspoon sugar

1 teaspoon paprika

¼ teaspoon garlic powder

¼ teaspoon cayenne pepper

¼ teaspoon cumin

1 teaspoon salt

¼ teaspoon black pepper

In a 4-quart slow cooker, add all ingredients. Cover and cook on low heat for 5 hours.

PER SERVING Calories: 170 | Fat: 3.5 g | Protein: 14 g | Sodium: 727 mg | Fiber: 5 g | Carbohydrates: 19 g | Sugar: 3 g

Simplify This Recipe

One way to simplify this recipe is to use a packet of fajita seasoning (sold in the international aisle in many stores) in place of the chili powder, sugar, paprika, garlic powder, cayenne pepper, cumin, salt, and black pepper.

Black Bean, Corn, and Fresh Tomato Chili

*Tofutti makes a delicious nondairy sour cream called Sour Supreme,
and it can be found in some national grocery store chains.*

INGREDIENTS | SERVES 4

1 red onion, diced

1 jalapeño, seeded and minced

3 cloves garlic, minced

1 (15-ounce) can black beans, drained

1 (15-ounce) can corn, drained

3 tablespoons chili powder

1 tablespoon paprika

1 teaspoon dried oregano

1 teaspoon ground cumin

½ teaspoon chipotle powder

2 cups Vegetable Broth (see Chapter 3)

1 teaspoon salt

¼ teaspoon black pepper

2 cups tomato, diced

¼ cup cilantro, chopped

4 tablespoons sour cream or vegan sour cream

1. In a 4-quart slow cooker, add all ingredients except tomatoes, cilantro, and sour cream. Cover and cook on low heat for 5 hours.

2. When the chili is done cooking, mix in the tomatoes and garnish with the cilantro. Top with sour cream or vegan sour cream.

PER SERVING Calories: 302 | Fat: 6 g | Protein: 12 g | Sodium: 1,023 mg | Fiber: 10 g | Carbohydrates: 42 g | Sugar: 8 g

Red Bean Chili

In the United States, "red beans" most commonly refers to kidney beans.

INGREDIENTS | SERVES 4

2 (15-ounce) cans red kidney beans, drained

½ cup onion, diced

2 cloves garlic, minced

2 cups Vegetable Broth (see Chapter 3)

1 tablespoon chili powder

½ tablespoon chipotle powder

½ tablespoon cumin

½ tablespoon paprika

1 (15-ounce) can tomatoes, diced

1 teaspoon salt

¼ teaspoon black pepper

In a 4-quart slow cooker, add all ingredients. Cover and cook on low heat for 5 hours.

PER SERVING Calories: 298 | Fat: 3 g | Protein: 12 g | Sodium: 860 mg | Fiber: 13 g | Carbohydrates: 38 g | Sugar: 8 g

The Benefits of Canned Tomatoes

In addition to being inexpensive and always available, canned tomatoes are higher in lycopene than fresh tomatoes, making them a great option for chili and stews.

Lentil Chili

Before using dried lentils, rinse them well and pick through to remove any debris or undesirable pieces.

INGREDIENTS | SERVES 6

1 cup lentils, uncooked

1 onion, diced

3 cloves garlic, minced

4 cups Vegetable Broth (see Chapter 3)

¼ cup tomato paste

1 cup carrots, chopped

1 cup celery, chopped

1 (15-ounce) can diced tomatoes, drained

2 tablespoons chili powder

½ tablespoon paprika

1 teaspoon dried oregano

1 teaspoon cumin

1 teaspoon salt

¼ teaspoon black pepper

In a 4-quart slow cooker, add all ingredients. Cover and cook on low heat for 8 hours.

PER SERVING Calories: 199 | Fat: 1 g | Protein: 11 g | Sodium: 688 mg | Fiber: 15 g | Carbohydrates: 38 g | Sugar: 10 g

Garden Vegetable Chili

A true garden vegetable recipe requires some flexibility, since all ingredients aren't available year round, and you should use what's actually growing in your garden.

INGREDIENTS | SERVES 8

1 large onion, diced

3 cloves garlic, minced

1 large green bell pepper, chopped

2 cups zucchini, chopped

1½ cups corn kernels

1 (28-ounce) can diced tomatoes

2 cups Vegetable Broth (see Chapter 3)

1 (15-ounce) can kidney beans, drained

1 (15-ounce) can pinto beans, drained

1 (15-ounce) can cannellini beans, drained

2 tablespoons chili powder

1 teaspoon cumin

1 teaspoon dried oregano

1 teaspoon salt

¼ teaspoon black pepper

In a 4-quart slow cooker, add all ingredients. Cover and cook on low heat for 6 hours.

PER SERVING Calories: 229 | Fat: 2.5 g | Protein: 10 g | Sodium: 648 mg | Fiber: 10 g | Carbohydrates: 35 g | Sugar: 5.5 g

Selecting What's in Season

In the summer, bell peppers, corn, green beans, and okra are in season and would be delicious additions to this recipe. In the winter, cauliflower, parsnips and winter squash may be in season and would be good, too.

Black Bean and "Sausage" Chili

Gimme Lean is a brand of vegan sausage that is sold in major grocery store chains and is usually found in the produce section.

INGREDIENTS | SERVES 6

1 red onion, diced

1 jalapeño, seeded and minced

2 carrots, peeled and chopped

3 cloves garlic, minced

1 (15-ounce) can black beans, drained

1 (14-ounce) package Gimme Lean Sausage, crumbled

3 tablespoons chili powder

1 tablespoon paprika

1 teaspoon dried thyme

1 teaspoon ground cumin

½ teaspoon chipotle powder

1 (28-ounce) can diced tomatoes, drained

2 cups Vegetable Broth (see Chapter 3)

1 teaspoon salt

¼ teaspoon black pepper

In a 4-quart slow cooker, add all ingredients. Cover and cook on low heat for 5 hours.

PER SERVING Calories: 331 | Fat: 19 g | Protein: 16 g | Sodium: 1,286 mg | Fiber: 9 g | Carbohydrates: 26 g | Sugar: 9 g

Acorn Squash Chili

Acorn squash keeps its shape in this chili, giving it a chunky texture.

INGREDIENTS | SERVES 8

2 cups acorn squash, cubed

2 (15-ounce) cans petite diced tomatoes

2 stalks celery, diced

1 medium onion, diced

3 cloves garlic, minced

2 carrots, diced

1 teaspoon mesquite liquid smoke

2 teaspoons hot sauce

1 teaspoon chili powder

1 teaspoon paprika

1 teaspoon oregano

1 teaspoon smoked paprika

1 (15-ounce) can kidney beans, drained and rinsed

1 (15-ounce) can cannellini beans, drained and rinsed

1 cup fresh corn kernels

1. In a 4-quart slow cooker, add all ingredients except the corn. Cover and cook for 8 hours on low.

2. Add the corn and stir. Cover and continue to cook on low for 30 minutes. Stir before serving.

PER SERVING Calories: 170 | Fat: 1.5 g | Protein: 8 g | Sodium: 417 mg | Fiber: 9 g | Carbohydrates: 32 g | Sugar: 6 g

Summer Chili

This chili is full of summer vegetables, and you can add vegetarian chicken for a heartier dish.

INGREDIENTS | SERVES 8

1 bulb fennel, diced
4 radishes, diced
2 stalks celery including leaves, diced
2 carrots, cut into coin-sized pieces
1 medium onion, diced
1 shallot, diced
4 cloves garlic, sliced
1 habanero pepper, diced
1 (15-ounce) can cannellini beans, drained and rinsed
1 (12-ounce) can tomato paste
½ teaspoon dried oregano
½ teaspoon black pepper
½ teaspoon crushed rosemary
½ teaspoon cayenne
½ teaspoon ground chipotle
1 teaspoon chili powder
1 teaspoon tarragon
¼ teaspoon cumin
¼ teaspoon celery seed
2 zucchini, cubed
10 Campari tomatoes, quartered
1 cup corn kernels

1. In a 4-quart slow cooker, add the fennel, radishes, celery, carrots, onion, shallot, garlic, habanero, beans, tomato paste, and all spices; stir. Cook on low for 6–7 hours.

2. Stir in the zucchini, tomatoes, and corn. Cook for an additional 30 minutes on high. Stir before serving.

PER SERVING Calories: 187 | Fat: 2 g | Protein: 7 g | Sodium: 532 mg | Fiber: 8 g | Carbohydrates: 31 g | Sugar: 10 g

Campari Tomatoes

Campari is a brand of tomatoes that are grown on the vine and have a sweet, juicy taste. They are round and on the small side, but not as small as cherry tomatoes.

CHAPTER 6

Sauces

Slow-Roasted Garlic and Tomato Sauce

Canned, diced tomatoes are a good substitute for fresh,
vine-ripened tomatoes when fresh tomatoes are not in season.

INGREDIENTS | YIELDS 4 CUPS

2 tablespoons olive oil

2½ pounds fresh, vine-ripened tomatoes, peeled and diced

1 teaspoon dried parsley

1 teaspoon dried basil

1 tablespoon balsamic vinegar

½ teaspoon granulated cane sugar

Salt, to taste

Freshly ground black pepper, to taste

3 heads roasted garlic, cloves removed from peel

In a 4-quart slow cooker, add all ingredients. Cover and cook on low for 3–4 hours.

PER SERVING (½ CUP) Calories: 175 | Fat: 7.5 g | Protein: 5.2 g | Sodium: 21.5 mg | Fiber: 4 g | Carbohydrates: 25.5 g | Sugar: 8 g

Roasting Garlic

Roast whole heads of garlic by cutting off the top ¼, drizzling with olive oil, and then wrapping in aluminum foil. Cook in an oven preheated to 400°F for about 45 minutes.

Vegan Alfredo

Top cooked fettuccine with this updated version of a classic sauce.

INGREDIENTS | SERVES 8

1 cup raw cashews

1 cup water

½ cup unsweetened soymilk

3 cups Vegetable Broth (see Chapter 3)

Juice of ½ lemon

½ cup nutritional yeast

1 teaspoon mustard

2 cloves garlic, minced

2 teaspoons salt

1 teaspoon pepper

1. In a blender, place the cashews, water, and soymilk. Process until very smooth.

2. In a 4-quart slow cooker, pour the blended cashew sauce and all remaining ingredients and stir well. Cover and cook over low heat for 1 hour.

PER SERVING Calories: 185.5 | Fat: 12.6 g | Protein: 6.3 g | Sodium: 638 mg | Fiber: 2 g | Carbohydrates: 14 g | Sugar: 4 g

Cooking with Cashews

Cashews are an excellent ingredient to use when you want to create a creamy vegan dish, but be sure to use raw cashews, not roasted or cooked in any other way. Also, remember that nuts are high in calories and fat, so they should be consumed in small quantities.

Jalapeño-Tomatillo Sauce

Serve this sauce over rice or in burritos or tacos.

INGREDIENTS | SERVES 4

1 teaspoon canola oil
2 cloves garlic, minced
1 onion, sliced
7 tomatillos, diced
2 jalapeños, minced
½ cup water

1. In a nonstick pan, heat the oil. Add the garlic, onion, tomatillos, and jalapeños and sauté about 5 minutes.

2. In a 4-quart slow cooker, place the mixture; add the water and stir. Cover and cook on low for 8 hours.

PER SERVING Calories: 50 | Fat: 2 g | Protein: 1 g | Sodium: 0 mg | Fiber: 2 g | Carbohydrates: 6 g | Sugar: 3 g

Lemon Dill Sauce

Tofu, pasta, or crisp vegetables such as asparagus make a great vehicle for this sauce.

INGREDIENTS | SERVES 4

2 cups Vegetable Broth (see Chapter 3)
½ cup lemon juice
½ cup fresh dill, chopped
1 teaspoon salt
¼ teaspoon white pepper

In a 2- or 4-quart slow cooker, place all ingredients. Cook on high, uncovered, for 3 hours.

PER SERVING Calories: 33 | Fat: 0 g | Protein: 1 g | Sodium: 635 mg | Fiber: 2 g | Carbohydrates: 8 g | Sugar: 3.6 g

A Peek at Peppercorns

Black peppercorns are the mature fruit of the black pepper plant, which grows in tropical areas. Green peppercorns are the immature fruit of the pepper plant. White peppercorns are mature black peppercorns with the black husks removed. Pink peppercorns are the dried berries of the Brazilian pepper.

Creamy Dijon Sauce

Dijon mustard is best in this recipe, but other varieties of high-quality mustard will work well, too.

INGREDIENTS | YIELDS 2 CUPS

1 tablespoon butter or vegan margarine
1 tablespoon flour
1 cup unsweetened soymilk
½ cup white wine
½ cup Vegetable Broth (see Chapter 3)
2 tablespoons Dijon mustard
¼ cup chopped shallots
½ teaspoon salt
½ teaspoon pepper

1. In the bottom of a 2-quart slow cooker, melt the butter or margarine. Stir in the flour to form a roux.

2. Whisk in the soymilk, white wine, and Vegetable Broth and stir until there are no lumps and it is well combined.

3. Add all remaining ingredients. Cover and cook over low heat for 3 hours.

PER SERVING (½ CUP) Calories: 102 | Fat: 4.3 g | Protein: 3 g | Sodium: 426 mg | Fiber: 1 g | Carbohydrates: 8 g | Sugar: 3.5 g

Country White Gravy

Kick this gravy up a notch by adding pieces of cooked vegetarian sausage crumbles just before serving.

INGREDIENTS | SERVES 8

½ cup vegetable oil

¼ cup onion, diced

3 cloves garlic, minced

½ cup flour

4 teaspoons nutritional yeast

4 tablespoons soy sauce

2 cups water

½ teaspoon dried sage

½ teaspoon salt

¼ teaspoon pepper

1. In a small sauce pan, heat the oil over medium-low heat. Add the onions and garlic and sauté for 2 minutes.

2. Transfer the oil mixture to a 4-quart slow cooker over low heat.

3. Stir in the flour to make a roux, then gradually add the nutritional yeast, soy sauce, and water, stirring constantly.

4. Add the sage, salt, and pepper, then cover, and cook for 1 hour.

PER SERVING Calories: 46 | Fat: 0 g | Protein: 2 g | Sodium: 605 mg | Fiber: 1 g | Carbohydrates: 9 g | Sugar: 1 g

Puttanesca Sauce

You can easily omit the anchovies found in the recipes for many puttanesca sauces and replace it with olive brine, the liquid that olives are packed in.

INGREDIENTS | SERVES 6

1 tablespoon olive oil

4 cloves garlic, minced

1 onion, diced

1 cup sliced black olives

1 tablespoon olive brine

28 ounces crushed tomatoes

1 (15-ounce) can diced tomatoes

1 tablespoon crushed red pepper

2 tablespoons drained nonpareil-sized capers

2 tablespoons fresh basil, chopped

What Is Sautéing?

Sautéing is a method of cooking that uses a small amount of fat to cook food in a shallow pan over medium-high heat. The goal is to brown the food while preserving its color, moisture, and flavor.

1. In a large sauté pan, heat the olive oil over medium heat. Add the garlic and onion and sauté until soft, about 3–4 minutes.

2. In a 4-quart slow cooker, place the onions and garlic; add the remaining ingredients. Stir to distribute the ingredients evenly.

3. Cook on low for 4–6 hours. If the sauce looks very wet at the end of the cooking time, remove the lid and cook on high for 15–30 minutes before serving.

PER SERVING Calories: 115 | Fat: 7.5 g | Protein: 2 g | Sodium: 388 mg | Fiber: 3.7 g | Carbohydrates: 12 g | Sugar: 6 g

Barbecue Sauce

Barbecue recipes vary greatly from region to region in the United States, so feel free to customize this one in order to please your taste buds.

INGREDIENTS | YIELDS 5 CUPS

4 cups ketchup

¼ cup soy sauce

¼ cup maple syrup

¼ cup prepared mustard

2 tablespoons apple cider vinegar

1 tablespoon liquid smoke

2 teaspoons chipotle powder

1 teaspoon dried thyme

1 teaspoon sweet paprika

1 teaspoon garlic powder

1 teaspoon cumin

In a 4-quart slow cooker, add all ingredients and stir well. Cover and cook on low for 4–6 hours.

PER SERVING (½ CUP) Calories: 126 | Fat: 1 g | Protein: 2.5 g | Sodium: 1,506 mg | Fiber: 1 g | Carbohydrates: 31 g | Sugar: 27 g

Mole

*Just like barbecue sauce in the United States, mole sauce recipes
vary greatly by region, and no two are exactly the same.*

INGREDIENTS | YIELDS 2 CUPS

2 tablespoons olive oil

½ onion, finely diced

3 garlic cloves, minced

1 teaspoon ground cumin

¼ teaspoon ground cinnamon

¼ teaspoon ground coriander

1 tablespoon chili powder

2 chipotles in adobo, seeded and minced

1 teaspoon salt

4 cups Vegetable Broth (see Chapter 3)

1 ounce vegan dark chocolate, chopped

1. In a sauté pan over medium heat, add the oil, onion, and garlic and sauté about 3 minutes. Add the cumin, cinnamon, and coriander and sauté for 1 minute.

2. Transfer the sautéed mixture to a 4-quart slow cooker. Add the chili powder, chipotles, and salt, then whish in the Vegetable Broth. Finally, add the chocolate.

3. Cover and cook over medium heat for 2 hours.

PER SERVING (½ CUP) Calories: 163 | Fat: 9.6 g | Protein: 2 g | Sodium: 688 mg | Fiber: 4.5 g | Carbohydrates: 20 g | Sugar: 10 g

Raspberry Coulis

A coulis is a thick sauce made from puréed fruits or vegetables. In this recipe, the slow cooking eliminates the need for puréeing because the fruit cooks down enough that straining is unnecessary.

INGREDIENTS | SERVES 8

12 ounces fresh or frozen raspberries

1 teaspoon balsamic vinegar

2 tablespoons sugar

Taste, Taste, Taste

When using fresh berries, it is important to taste them prior to sweetening. One batch of berries might be tart while the next might be very sweet. Reduce or eliminate extra sugar if using very ripe, sweet berries.

1. In a 2-quart slow cooker, place all ingredients. Mash gently with a potato masher.

2. Cook on low for 4 hours, uncovered. Stir before serving.

PER SERVING Calories: 35 | Fat: 0 g | Protein: 1 g | Sodium: 0 mg | Fiber: 3 g | Carbohydrates: 8 g | Sugar: 4 g

Homemade Ketchup

Why buy bottled when homemade ketchup is this easy?

INGREDIENTS | SERVES 32

1 (15-ounce) can no-salt-added tomato sauce

2 teaspoons water

½ teaspoon onion powder

½ cup sugar

⅓ cup cider vinegar

¼ teaspoon sea salt

¼ teaspoon ground cinnamon

⅛ teaspoon ground cloves

Pinch ground allspice

Pinch nutmeg

Pinch freshly ground pepper

⅔ teaspoon sweet paprika

1. In a 2-quart slow cooker, add all ingredients except paprika. Cover and cook for 2–4 hours, or until ketchup reaches desired consistency, stirring occasionally.

2. Turn off the slow cooker or remove the crock from the slow cooker and stir in the paprika.

3. Allow mixture to cool, then put in a covered container (such as a recycled ketchup bottle). Store in the refrigerator until needed.

PER SERVING Calories: 18 | Fat: 0 g | Protein: 0 g | Sodium: 71 mg | Fiber: 0 g | Carbohydrates: 4 g | Sugar: 4 g

Ketchup with a Kick

If you like zesty ketchup, you can add crushed red peppers, cayenne pepper, or salt-free chili powder along with, or instead of, the cinnamon and other seasonings. Another alternative is to use hot paprika rather than sweet paprika.

Coconut Curry Sauce

Red curry paste is ideal for this recipe, but any variety will do.

INGREDIENTS | YIELDS ABOUT 2 CUPS

1 (14-ounce) can coconut milk

1 cup Vegetable Broth (see Chapter 3)

1 teaspoon soy sauce

1 tablespoon curry paste

1 tablespoon lime juice

2 cloves garlic, minced

½ teaspoon salt

¼ cup chopped cilantro

1. In a 4-quart slow cooker, add all ingredients except cilantro. Cover and cook on low heat for 2 hours.

2. Add the chopped cilantro and cook for an additional 30 minutes.

PER SERVING (½ CUP) Calories: 214 | Fat: 21 g | Protein: 2.7 g | Sodium: 402 mg | Fiber: 1 g | Carbohydrates: 7 g | Sugar: 1.5 g

White Wine–Garlic Sauce

It's a myth that all alcohol is removed from a dish when cooked,
so avoid this sauce if you abstain from drinking.

INGREDIENTS | YIELDS 2 CUPS

6 tablespoons butter or vegan margarine

2 tablespoons shallot, minced

5 cloves garlic, minced

1 cup white wine

1 cup Vegetable Broth (see Chapter 3)

1½ teaspoons salt

Which Wine?

As a general rule, if you wouldn't drink it, then don't cook with it, and remember to consider how the flavor of the wine will pair with other ingredients. If you are trying to achieve a rich, earthy sauce, then don't use a floral or fruity white. Instead, choose an oaky chardonnay.

1. In a sauté pan, melt the butter or margarine over medium heat. Add the shallot and garlic and sauté for 2 minutes.

2. Add the sautéed blend to a 4-quart slow cooker. Add all remaining ingredients, stir, and cook on low for 2 hours.

PER SERVING (½ CUP) Calories: 223 | Fat: 17 g | Protein: 1 g | Sodium: 910 mg | Fiber: 1 g | Carbohydrates: 6.6 g | Sugar: 2 g

Three-Pepper Sauce

Cayenne peppers are most commonly found dried and ground in the herbs and spices isle of your grocery store.

INGREDIENTS | SERVES 4

1 (28-ounce) can diced tomatoes

2 tablespoons tomato paste

1 red bell pepper, finely diced

1 green bell pepper, finely diced

½ red onion, diced

3 cloves garlic, minced

1 teaspoon cayenne pepper

½ teaspoon sugar

½ teaspoon salt

In a 4-quart slow cooker, add all ingredients. Cover and cook on low heat for 6–8 hours.

PER SERVING Calories: 59 | Fat: 0.5 g | Protein: 2.6 g | Sodium: 307 mg | Fiber: 3.8 g | Carbohydrates: 13 g | Sugar: 7.8 g

Easy Peanut Sauce

Choose a peanut butter that is free of added flavors and is as natural as possible, so that it won't distort the flavors in your dish.

INGREDIENTS | YIELDS 3 CUPS

1 cup smooth peanut butter

4 tablespoons maple syrup

½ cup sesame oil

1 teaspoon cayenne pepper

1½ teaspoons cumin

1 teaspoon garlic powder

1½ teaspoons salt

2 cups water

1. In a blender, add all ingredients except for the water. Blend as you slowly add the water until you reach the desired consistency.

2. Pour the sauce into a 2-quart slow cooker and cook over low heat for 1 hour.

PER SERVING (½ CUP) Calories: 452 | Fat: 40 g | Protein: 11 g | Sodium: 792 mg | Fiber: 3 g | Carbohydrates: 18 g | Sugar: 12 g

Uses for Peanut Sauce

Peanut sauce can be used to dress Asian noodles such as udon or soba noodles. It may also be used as a dipping sauce for steamed broccoli or spring rolls.

CHAPTER 7

Vegetables

Herb-Stuffed Tomatoes

Serve these Italian-influenced stuffed tomatoes with a simple salad for an easy, light meal.

INGREDIENTS | SERVES 4

4 large tomatoes

1 cup cooked quinoa

1 stalk celery, minced

1 tablespoon fresh garlic, minced

2 tablespoons fresh oregano, minced

2 tablespoons fresh Italian parsley, minced

1 teaspoon dried chervil

1 teaspoon fennel seeds

¾ cup water

1. Cut out the core of each tomato and discard. Scoop out the seeds, leaving the walls of the tomato intact.

2. In a small bowl, stir together the quinoa, celery, garlic, and spices. Divide evenly among the 4 tomatoes.

3. Place the filled tomatoes in a single layer in an oval 4-quart slow cooker. Pour the water into the bottom of the slow cooker. Cook on low for 4 hours.

PER SERVING Calories: 191 | Fat: 2 g | Protein: 7 g | Sodium: 30 mg | Fiber: 4.5 g | Carbohydrates: 29 g | Sugar: 5 g

Homemade Sauerkraut

This isn't your traditional sauerkraut recipe, which requires fermentation, but is a delicious spin on the classic.

INGREDIENTS | SERVES 12

1 head cabbage, finely shredded

1 tablespoon kosher salt

Water, as needed

1 teaspoon sugar

1 sprig dill

1. Place the shredded cabbage in a 4- or 6-quart slow cooker and toss with the salt until juice from the cabbage begins to appear. Pack the cabbage down into the liquid, then fill with enough water to just cover the cabbage.

2. Add the sugar and dill and cook over low heat for 8–10 hours. Remove the dill before serving.

PER SERVING Calories: 20 | Fat: 0 g | Protein: 1 g | Sodium: 603 mg | Fiber: 2 g | Carbohydrates: 5 g | Sugar: 3 g

Veggie Dogs

There are many brands of vegetarian and vegan hot dogs for sale in grocery stores around the country, and you can even find them at WalMart. Use homemade sauerkraut as a topping for your dog.

Citrusy Beets

Beets can be served as a warm side dish or a chilled salad over a bed of greens.

INGREDIENTS | SERVES 4

12 baby beets, halved, ends trimmed
1 cup orange juice
Juice of ½ lime
¼ red onion, sliced
½ teaspoon pepper

Add all ingredients to a 2-quart or 4-quart slow cooker and cook on low for 4 hours.

PER SERVING Calories: 142 | Fat: 1 g | Protein: 5 g | Sodium: 194 mg | Fiber: 7.5 g | Carbohydrates: 32 g | Sugar: 22 g

Caramelized Onions

Caramelized onions are a great addition to roasts, dips, and sandwiches.

INGREDIENTS | YIELDS 1 QUART

4 pounds Vidalia or other sweet onions
3 tablespoons butter or vegan margarine
1 tablespoon balsamic vinegar

Storing Caramelized Onions

Store the onions in an airtight container. They will keep up to 2 weeks refrigerated or up to 6 months frozen. If frozen, defrost overnight in the refrigerator before using.

1. Peel and slice the onions in ¼-inch slices. Separate them into rings. Thinly slice the butter or margarine.

2. Place the onions into a 4-quart slow cooker. Scatter butter or margarine slices over top of the onions and drizzle with balsamic vinegar. Cover and cook on low for 10 hours.

3. If after 10 hours the onions are wet, turn the slow cooker up to high and cook uncovered for an additional 30 minutes, or until the liquid evaporates.

PER SERVING (2 TABLESPOONS) Calories: 35 | Fat: 1 g | Protein: 1 g | Sodium: 0 mg | Fiber: <1 g | Carbohydrates: 6 g | Sugar: 3 g

Corn on the Cob

Corn husks can be dried out and reused as a tamale casing.

INGREDIENTS | SERVES 6

6 ears corn, shucked
Water, as needed

Serving Suggestions

Plain corn on the cob can be delicious and juicy, but you can add even more flavor by topping it with butter or margarine, cayenne pepper, a cilantro-butter blend, or even curry!

1. Place the corn in a 4-quart slow cooker and cover with water until it is 1" from the top of the slow cooker.

2. Cook on high heat for 2 hours.

PER SERVING Calories: 122.5 | Fat: 1 g | Protein: 4 g | Sodium: 6 mg | Fiber: 3.5 g | Carbohydrates: 29 g | Sugar: 4.7 g

Creamed Corn

For this recipe, choose frozen corn that is free of salt or added flavors.

INGREDIENTS | SERVES 4

1 (16-ounce) bag frozen corn kernels
½ cup whole milk or unsweetened soymilk
¼ cup butter or vegan margarine
½ teaspoon salt
¼ teaspoon pepper

1. Add all ingredients to a 4-quart slow cooker. Cover and cook on high heat for 3 hours.

2. Allow to cool slightly, then pour ¼ of the corn into a blender and pulse 1–2 times. Return to the slow cooker and stir before serving.

PER SERVING Calories: 219 | Fat: 13 g | Protein: 4.5 g | Sodium: 313 mg | Fiber: 2.7 g | Carbohydrates: 1 g | Sugar: 1.6 g

"Steamed" Artichokes

Choose artichokes that are all the same size so they will finish cooking at the same time.

INGREDIENTS | SERVES 4

4 large artichokes
1 cup water
1 lemon, cut into eighths
2 tablespoons lemon juice
1 teaspoon dried oregano

1. Place the artichokes stem-side down in an oval 4-quart slow cooker. Pour the water into the bottom of the slow cooker. Add the lemons, lemon juice, and oregano.

2. Cook on low for 6 hours, or until the leaves are tender.

PER SERVING Calories: 80 | Fat: 0 g | Protein: 5 g | Sodium: 150 mg | Fiber: 9 g | Carbohydrates: 19 g | Sugar: 2 g

Eggplant Caponata

Serve this on small slices of Italian bread as an appetizer or use as a filling in sandwiches or wraps.

INGREDIENTS | SERVES 8

2 (1-pound) eggplants
1 teaspoon olive oil
1 red onion, diced
4 cloves garlic, minced
1 stalk celery, diced
2 tomatoes, diced
2 tablespoons nonpareil capers
2 tablespoons toasted pine nuts
1 teaspoon red pepper flakes
¼ cup red wine vinegar

1. Pierce the eggplants with a fork. Cook on high in a 4- or 6-quart slow cooker for 2 hours.

2. Allow to cool. Peel off the skin. Slice each in half and remove the seeds. Discard the skin and seeds.

3. Place the pulp in a food processor. Pulse until smooth. Set aside.

4. Heat the oil in a nonstick skillet. Sauté the onion, garlic, and celery until the onion is soft.

5. Add the eggplant and tomatoes. Sauté 3 minutes.

6. Return to the slow cooker and add the capers, pine nuts, red pepper flakes, and vinegar. Stir. Cook on low 30 minutes. Stir prior to serving.

PER SERVING Calories: 75 | Fat: 3 g | Protein: 2 g | Sodium: 75 mg | Fiber: 5 g | Carbohydrates: 11 g | Sugar: 4 g

Gingered Sweet Potatoes

For this festive recipe, look for candied ginger that is not coated in sugar; it's called uncrystallized ginger.

INGREDIENTS | SERVES 10

2½ pounds sweet potatoes

1 cup water

1 tablespoon grated fresh ginger

½ tablespoon minced uncrystallized candied ginger

½ tablespoon butter or vegan margarine

Sweet Potatoes or Yams?

Yams are not grown domestically, so the yams commonly found in supermarkets are actually varieties of sweet potato. True yams can be found in Asian or specialty stores and come in colors ranging from purple to yellow to white.

1. Peel and quarter the sweet potatoes. Add them to a 4-quart slow cooker. Add the water, fresh ginger, and candied ginger. Stir.

2. Cook on high for 3–4 hours, or until the potatoes are tender.

3. Add the butter or vegan margarine, and mash. Serve immediately, or turn them down to low to keep warm for up to 3 hours.

PER SERVING Calories: 100 | Fat: 0.5 g | Protein: 2 g | Sodium: 65 mg | Fiber: 3 g | Carbohydrates: 23 g | Sugar: 3 g

Ratatouille

Ratatouille made in the slow cooker comes out surprisingly crisp-tender.

INGREDIENTS | SERVES 4

1 onion, roughly chopped

1 eggplant, sliced horizontally

2 zucchini, sliced

1 cubanelle pepper, sliced

3 tomatoes, cut into wedges

2 tablespoons fresh basil, minced

2 tablespoons fresh Italian parsley, minced

¼ teaspoon salt

½ teaspoon freshly ground black pepper

3 ounces tomato paste

¼ cup water

1. Place the onion, eggplant, zucchini, pepper, and tomatoes into a 4-quart slow cooker. Sprinkle with basil, parsley, salt, and pepper.

2. In a small bowl, whisk the tomato paste and water together. Pour the mixture over the vegetables. Stir.

3. Cook on low for 4 hours, or until the eggplant and zucchini are fork-tender.

PER SERVING Calories: 110 | Fat: 1 g | Protein: 5 g | Sodium: 330 mg | Fiber: 8 g | Carbohydrates: 24 g | Sugar: 13 g

Rosemary-Thyme Green Beans

In this recipe, the slow cooker acts like a steamer, resulting in tender, crisp green beans.

INGREDIENTS | SERVES 4

1 pound green beans
1 tablespoon fresh minced rosemary
1 teaspoon fresh minced thyme
2 tablespoons lemon juice
2 tablespoons water

1. Place all ingredients into a 2-quart slow cooker. Stir to distribute the spices evenly.

2. Cook on low for 1½ hours, or until the green beans are tender. Stir before serving.

PER SERVING Calories: 40 | Fat: 0 g | Protein: 2 g | Sodium: 5 mg | Fiber: 4 g | Carbohydrates: 9 g | Sugar: 4 g

Spiced "Baked" Eggplant

Serve this as a main dish over rice or as a side dish as is.

INGREDIENTS | SERVES 4

1 pound eggplant, cubed
⅓ cup onion, sliced
½ teaspoon red pepper flakes
½ teaspoon crushed rosemary
¼ cup lemon juice

Place all ingredients in a 1½ to 2-quart slow cooker. Cook on low for 3 hours, or until the eggplant is tender.

PER SERVING Calories: 40 | Fat: 0 g | Protein: 1 g | Sodium: 6 mg | Fiber: 4 g | Carbohydrates: 9 g | Sugar: 3.5 g

Cold Snap

Take care not to put a cold ceramic slow cooker insert directly into the slow cooker. The sudden shift in temperature can cause it to crack. If you want to prepare your ingredients the night before use, refrigerate them in reusable containers, not in the insert.

Stewed Squash

Crisp and fresh, this is the perfect summer side dish to show off the season's bounty.

INGREDIENTS | SERVES 4

1 medium onion, cut into ¼" slices

3 cups sliced zucchini

1 tablespoon fresh dill

3 tablespoons lemon juice

¼ teaspoon salt

¼ teaspoon black pepper

¾ cup fresh corn kernels

1 teaspoon butter or vegan margarine

1. Place the onions on the bottom of a 1½- to 2-quart slow cooker. Top with zucchini, dill, lemon juice, salt, and pepper. Cook on low for 3½ hours.

2. Add the corn and butter or vegan margarine and stir. Cook for an additional 30 minutes on high.

PER SERVING Calories: 70 | Fat: 1.5 g | Protein: 2 g | Sodium: 160 mg | Fiber: 2 g | Carbohydrates: 14 g | Sugar: 5 g

Stewed Tomatoes

For an Italian variation, add basil and Italian parsley.

INGREDIENTS | SERVES 6

28 ounces whole tomatoes in purée, diced

1 tablespoon minced onion

1 stalk celery, diced

½ teaspoon oregano

½ teaspoon thyme

Place all ingredients into a 2-quart slow cooker. Stir. Cook on low up to 8 hours.

PER SERVING Calories: 25 | Fat: 0 g | Protein: 1 g | Sodium: 180 mg | Fiber: 1 g | Carbohydrates: 6 g | Sugar: 3 g

Tomato Varieties

Small tomatoes used in sauces such as Roma tomatoes or cherry tomatoes, are best for this recipe. Avoid large tomatoes that are used for their large slices, such as beefsteak.

Stuffed Eggplant

This easy vegan dish is a complete meal in itself.

INGREDIENTS | SERVES 2

1 (1-pound) eggplant
½ teaspoon olive oil
2 tablespoons red onion, minced
1 clove garlic, minced
⅓ cup cooked rice
1 tablespoon fresh parsley
¼ cup corn kernels
¼ cup diced crimini mushrooms
1 (15-ounce) can diced tomatoes with onions and garlic

1. Preheat oven to 375°F.

2. Slice the eggplant in 2 equal halves, lengthwise. Use an ice cream scoop to take out the seeds. Place on a baking sheet, skin-side down. Bake for 8 minutes. Allow to cool slightly.

3. In a small skillet, heat the oil. Add the onions and garlic and sauté until softened, about 3 minutes.

4. In a medium bowl, stir the onions, garlic, rice, parsley, corn, and mushrooms. Divide evenly between the eggplant halves.

5. Pour the tomatoes onto the bottom of an oval 4- or 6-quart slow cooker. Place the eggplant halves side by side on top of the tomatoes. Cook on low for 3 hours.

6. Remove the eggplants and plate. Drizzle with tomato sauce.

PER SERVING Calories: 190 | Fat: 3.5 g | Protein: 8 g | Sodium: 807 mg | Fiber: 10 g | Carbohydrates: 41 g | Sugar: 12 g

Zucchini Ragout

A ragout is either a main-dish stew or a sauce. This one can be served as either.

INGREDIENTS | SERVES 6

5 ounces fresh spinach

3 zucchini, diced

½ cup diced red onion

2 stalks celery, diced

2 carrots, diced

1 parsnip, diced

3 tablespoons tomato paste

¼ cup water

1 teaspoon freshly ground black pepper

¼ teaspoon kosher salt

1 tablespoon minced fresh basil

1 tablespoon minced fresh Italian parsley

1 tablespoon minced fresh oregano

Place all ingredients into a 4-quart slow cooker. Stir. Cook on low for 4 hours. Stir before serving.

PER SERVING Calories: 60 | Fat: 0 g | Protein: 2 g | Sodium: 220 mg | Fiber: 3 g | Carbohydrates: 10 g | Sugar: 3 g

Saving on Herbs

The cost of herbs can add up quickly, but you can save a little money by shopping at an international farmers market or buying a blend of spices (an Italian blend would work well in this recipe) instead of buying each individually.

Moroccan Root Vegetables

Moroccan Root Vegetables is good served with couscous and a yogurt or vegan side salad.

INGREDIENTS | SERVES 8

1 pound parsnips, peeled and diced

1 pound turnips, peeled and diced

2 medium onions, chopped

1 pound carrots, peeled and diced

6 dried apricots, chopped

4 pitted prunes, chopped

1 teaspoon ground turmeric

1 teaspoon ground cumin

½ teaspoon ground ginger

½ teaspoon ground cinnamon

¼ teaspoon ground cayenne pepper

1 tablespoon dried parsley

1 tablespoon dried cilantro

2 cups Vegetable Broth (see Chapter 3)

1 teaspoon salt

1. Add the parsnips, turnips, onions, carrots, apricots, prunes, turmeric, cumin, ginger, cinnamon, cayenne pepper, parsley, and cilantro to a 4-quart slow cooker.

2. Pour in the Vegetable Broth and salt.

3. Cover and cook on low for 9 hours, or until the vegetables are cooked through.

PER SERVING Calories: 125 | Fat: 0.6 g | Protein: 2.7 g | Sodium: 399 mg | Fiber: 6 g | Carbohydrates: 30 g | Sugar: 14 g

Meatless Moussaka

If you get your eggplant at the supermarket and suspect that it's been waxed, peel it before dicing it and adding it to the slow cooker.

INGREDIENTS | SERVES 8

¾ cup dry brown or yellow lentils, rinsed and drained

2 large potatoes, peeled and diced

1 cup water

1 stalk celery, diced fine

1 medium sweet onion, peeled and diced

3 cloves of garlic, minced

½ teaspoon salt

¼ teaspoon ground cinnamon

Pinch freshly ground nutmeg

¼ teaspoon freshly ground black pepper

¼ teaspoon dried basil

¼ teaspoon dried oregano

¼ teaspoon dried parsley

1 medium eggplant, diced

12 baby carrots, each cut into 3 pieces

1 (14½-ounce) can diced tomatoes

1 (8-ounce) package cream cheese or vegan cream cheese, softened

1. Add the lentils, potatoes, water, celery, onion, garlic, salt, cinnamon, nutmeg, pepper, basil, oregano, and parsley to a 4-quart slow cooker. Stir. Top with eggplant and carrots.

2. Cover and cook on low for 6 hours, or until the lentils are cooked through.

3. Stir in undrained tomatoes and add a dollop of cream cheese over lentil mixture. Cover, and cook on low for an additional 30 minutes.

PER SERVING Calories: 235 | Fat: 10 g | Protein: 8.6 g | Sodium: 333 mg | Fiber: 7 g | Carbohydrates: 29 g | Sugar: 6 g

Curried Cauliflower

Heating herbs and spices before adding them to water intensifies the flavor.

INGREDIENTS | SERVES 6

1 tablespoon olive oil
¼ cup finely diced onion
1½ teaspoons curry powder
½ teaspoon cumin
½ teaspoon coriander
1 teaspoon chili powder
1 teaspoon salt
1 cup diced tomatoes
1 cup water
1 head cauliflower, chopped

1. Heat the olive oil in the bottom of a 4-quart slow cooker set to medium heat. Add the onion and cook for 5 minutes.

2. Add the curry powder, cumin, coriander, chili powder, salt, and tomatoes and stir until well combined.

3. Add the water and cauliflower to the spice mixture in the slow cooker and stir until the cauliflower is coated. Cover and cook over medium heat for about 3 hours.

PER SERVING Calories: 56 | Fat: 3 g | Protein: 2 g | Sodium: 430 mg | Fiber: 3 g | Carbohydrates: 7 g | Sugar: 3 g

Mushroom and Olive Blend

Try serving on top of toasted baguette slices or on pasta or as a savory side dish.

INGREDIENTS | SERVES 6

2 tablespoons butter or vegan margarine

1 clove garlic, minced

½ cup sliced shiitake mushrooms

½ cup sliced oyster mushrooms

½ cup chopped hen of the woods mushrooms

¼ cup pitted and sliced kalamata olives

½ teaspoon salt

¼ teaspoon pepper

Mushroom Varieties

Hen of the woods mushrooms are also called maitake mushrooms, and grow in clusters. If you can't find this variety, you can substitute ½ cup more shiitake or oyster mushrooms.

Add all ingredients to a 2-quart slow cooker, cover and cook on low heat for 2 hours. Stir occasionally to make sure the butter or margarine is coating the mushrooms.

PER SERVING Calories: 44 | Fat: 4 g | Protein: 0.7 g | Sodium: 199 mg | Fiber: 1 g | Carbohydrates: 2 g | Sugar: 0.4 g

Cranberry-Walnut Brussels Sprouts

The combination of cranberries and walnuts makes this a perfect Thanksgiving side dish.

INGREDIENTS | SERVES 6

1 pound Brussels sprouts, trimmed and quartered

2 tablespoons olive oil

2 tablespoons water

½ teaspoon salt

¼ teaspoon pepper

¼ cup dried cranberries

¼ cup walnuts, chopped

1. Place all ingredients in a 2-quart slow cooker, stir until the olive oil coats the other ingredients.

2. Cover and cook on high heat for 2½ hours.

PER SERVING Calories: 87 | Fat: 8 g | Protein: 0.8 g | Sodium: 197 mg | Fiber: 2 g | Carbohydrates: 5 g | Sugar: 3 g

Baby Bok Choy

Bok choy is also known as Chinese cabbage.
Baby bok choy is simply a smaller, more tender version of mature bok choy.

INGREDIENTS | SERVES 6

2 tablespoons soy sauce

2 tablespoons apple cider vinegar

2 tablespoons sesame oil

½ teaspoon garlic powder

1 teaspoon crushed red pepper flakes

3 heads baby bok choy, halved lengthwise

1. In a small bowl, whisk together all ingredients except for the bok choy.

2. Place the bok choy in a 4-quart slow cooker, pour the soy sauce mixture over the bok choy. Cover and cook on low heat for 3 hours.

PER SERVING Calories: 102 | Fat: 5 g | Protein: 7 g | Sodium: 573 mg | Fiber: 3 g | Carbohydrates: 10 g | Sugar: 5.6 g

Cheesy Poblano Peppers

Poblanos are a mild pepper often used in chile rellenos.
Due to their thickness, these large, heart-shaped peppers are great for stuffing.

INGREDIENTS | SERVES 4

1 tablespoon olive oil

1 clove garlic, minced

¼ cup diced onion

4 poblano peppers, seeded and sliced into 1" rings

1 cup potatoes, peeled and diced into cubes

½ cup 2% milk or unsweetened soymilk

½ cup shredded Cheddar cheese or vegan Cheddar cheese

½ teaspoon salt

1. In a large sauté pan over medium heat, heat the olive oil. Add the garlic and onion and sauté for 2 minutes. Add the sliced poblano rings and sauté for 2 more minutes.

2. Pour the sautéed poblano mixture into a 4-quart slow cooker, then add the potato, milk or soymilk, cheese, and salt. Stir.

3. Cover and cook over low heat for 7–8 hours.

PER SERVING Calories: 149 | Fat: 8.6 g | Protein: 6 g | Sodium: 403 mg | Fiber: 2 g | Carbohydrates: 13 g | Sugar: 5 g

Variations

One variation for this recipe is to use the cooked garlic, onion, potato, soymilk, cheese, and salt as a soft mashed filling for whole poblanos. You could bake them or batter and fry them to perfection!

Vegan Creamed Spinach

Fresh spinach reduces greatly when cooked, so to get a bigger bang for your buck, use frozen spinach when possible.

INGREDIENTS | SERVES 6

1 tablespoon vegan margarine
1 clove garlic, minced
1 tablespoon flour
1 cup unsweetened soymilk
½ teaspoon salt
½ crushed teaspoon red pepper
¼ teaspoon dried sage
1 (12-ounce) package frozen spinach, thawed

1. Melt the margarine in a 2-quart slow cooker over medium heat. Add the garlic, and cook for 2 minutes before stirring in the flour.

2. Slowly pour in the soymilk and whisk until all lumps are removed.

3. Add all remaining ingredients. Stir, and cook over low heat for 1–2 hours.

PER SERVING Calories: 61 | Fat: 3 g | Protein: 3.6 g | Sodium: 281 mg | Fiber: 2 g | Carbohydrates: 6 g | Sugar: 2 g

Variations

You can simplify this recipe by going with a simple butter or margarine sauce that is flavored with salt, pepper, and sage or make this savory dish even richer by adding a sprinkling of vegan cheese such as Daiya Mozzarella Style Shreds.

Parsnip Purée

Parsnips are long white root vegetables related to carrots.
Due to the starchiness of their texture, they can frequently be used in place of potatoes.

INGREDIENTS | SERVES 6

5 medium parsnips, peeled and chopped
½ cup Vegetable Broth (see Chapter 3)
½ cup 2% milk or unsweetened soymilk
1 teaspoon salt
1 tablespoon butter or vegan margarine

1. Add the parsnips, Vegetable Broth, milk, and salt to a 4-quart slow cooker. Cover, and cook over low heat for 4 hours.

2. Allow the parsnips to cool slightly, then use an immersion blender to process, or use a blender or food processor and blend in batches.

3. Return to the slow cooker, add the butter or margarine, and heat until melted.

PER SERVING Calories: 51 | Fat: 2.6 g | Protein: 1 g | Sodium: 411 mg | Fiber: 1.4 g | Carbohydrates: 6 g | Sugar: 2.7 g

CHAPTER 8

Potatoes

Potato Messaround

"Messaround" means a little bit of everything, which is what this recipe has! Try playing with it by adding different cheeses and peppers or swap out the broth and soup, to your taste.

INGREDIENTS | SERVES 4

8 cups red potatoes, cubed

1 red onion, diced

1 poblano pepper, diced

1 red pepper, diced

1 jalepeño pepper, minced

3 cups vegetarian "chicken" broth

1 (14.5-ounce) can cream of mushroom soup or vegan cream of mushroom soup

1 teaspoon salt

¼ teaspoon black pepper

1 cup shredded Cheddar cheese or vegan Cheddar

2 tablespoons chives

1. Add all of the ingredients to a 4-quart slow cooker except for the chives.

2. Cover and cook on medium-high heat for 4–5 hours. Garnish with the chives.

PER SERVING Calories: 407 | Fat: 18 g | Protein: 16 g | Sodium: 926 mg | Fiber: 5 g | Carbohydrates: 59 g | Sugar: 6 g

Make It Vegan

Make vegan cream of mushroom soup by adding 2 tablespoons of a light roux to 2 cups unsweetened soymilk, then adding sautéed mushrooms and onions.

Sweet Potato Casserole

If you'd like to use fresh sweet potatoes in this casserole, steam or roast them before using in the dish.

INGREDIENTS | SERVES 4

2 (18-ounce) cans sweet potatoes, drained and slightly mashed

1 cup unsweetened soymilk

½ cup butter or vegan margarine, melted

½ cup white sugar

1 teaspoon cinnamon

½ teaspoon nutmeg

½ cup pecans, chopped

½ cup brown sugar

2 tablespoons flour

1. Add the mashed sweet potatoes, soymilk, ¼ cup of butter or vegan margarine, sugar, cinnamon, and nutmeg to a 4-quart slow cooker.

2. In a bowl, mix the pecans, brown sugar, flour, and remaining ¼ cup of butter or margarine.

3. Pour the mixture over the top of the casserole. Cover and cook on medium-high heat for 4–5 hours.

PER SERVING Calories: 666 | Fat: 34 g | Protein: 8 g | Sodium: 181 mg | Fiber: 10 g | Carbohydrates: 96 g | Sugar: 64 g

Potatoes Paprikash

This Hungarian classic is the perfect spicy side dish to serve with a seitan roast.

INGREDIENTS | SERVES 8

1½ teaspoons olive oil

1 medium onion, halved and sliced

1 shallot, minced

4 cloves garlic, minced

½ teaspoon salt

½ teaspoon caraway seeds

¼ teaspoon freshly ground black pepper

1 teaspoon cayenne

3 tablespoons paprika

2 pounds red skin potatoes, thinly sliced

2 cups Vegetable Broth (see Chapter 3)

2 tablespoons tomato paste

½ cup reduced-fat sour cream or vegan sour cream

1. In a nonstick pan, heat the oil. Add the onion, shallot, and garlic and sauté for 1–2 minutes, or until they begin to soften. Add the salt, caraway seeds, pepper, cayenne, and paprika, and stir. Immediately remove from heat.

2. Add the onion mixture, potatoes, broth, and tomato paste to a 4-quart slow cooker. Stir to coat the potatoes evenly.

3. Cover and cook on high for 2½ hours, or until the potatoes are tender.

4. Turn off the heat and stir in the sour cream.

PER SERVING Calories: 189 | Fat: 3 g | Protein: 4 g | Sodium: 612 mg | Fiber: 4 g | Carbohydrates: 26 g | Sugar: 4 g

Hungarian Cuisine

Hungarian food is very aromatic and can be quite heavy. It's most famous dishes are goulash, a meat and vegetable soup or stew, and paprikash.

Rosemary-Garlic Mashed Potatoes

Slow-cooked mashed potatoes are the perfect side for busy holiday cooks. Not only does this dish leave a burner free for other cooking, there is no need to boil the potatoes before mashing them.

INGREDIENTS | SERVES 10

3 pounds red skin potatoes, quartered

4 cloves garlic, minced

¾ cup Vegetable Broth (see Chapter 3)

1 tablespoon minced, fresh rosemary

2 teaspoons salt

¼ cup 1% milk or unsweetened soymilk

1 tablespoon butter or vegan margarine

⅓ cup reduced-fat sour cream or vegan sour cream

1. Place the potatoes in a 4-quart slow cooker. Add garlic, broth, rosemary, and salt. Stir.

2. Cover and cook on high until potatoes are tender, about 3–4 hours.

3. Pour in milk, butter, and sour cream or the vegan alternatives. Mash with a potato masher.

PER SERVING Calories: 124 | Fat: 2.4 g | Protein: 3 g | Sodium: 492 mg | Fiber: 3 g | Carbohydrates: 23 g | Sugar: 2 g

Southwestern Casserole

Unless you're vegan, serve this delicious dish with a poached egg on top.

INGREDIENTS | SERVES 6

4 large red potatoes, diced

1 (15-ounce) can black beans, drained

1 large onion, diced

1 jalapeño, seeded and diced

1 tablespoon butter or vegan margarine

1 (15-ounce) can diced tomatoes

4 ounces button mushrooms, sliced

¼ teaspoon salt

¼ teaspoon pepper

¼ cup shredded Mexican-blend cheese or vegan Cheddar

1. In a 4-quart slow cooker, stir all ingredients together except the cheese.

2. Cover and cook on low for 8–9 hours.

3. Stir in the cheese shortly before serving.

PER SERVING Calories: 217 | Fat: 4 g | Protein: 9 g | Sodium: 445 mg | Fiber: 6 g | Carbohydrates: 38 g | Sugar: 6 g

Vegan Cheddar

There are several varieties of vegan Cheddar cheese for sale in grocery stores around the country, but the one that melts, stretches, and tastes the best is Daiya's Cheddar Style Shreds.

Cheesy Peasy Potatoes

Cheese, potatoes, and peas are a classic dinner combo! Use whatever variety of potato you like most, and if you don't like mushrooms, feel free to use cream of celery soup instead.

INGREDIENTS | SERVES 4

8 cups potatoes, cubed

1 (14.5-ounce) can cream of mushroom soup or vegan cream of mushroom soup

3 cups vegetarian "chicken" broth

2 cups frozen peas

1 cup chopped vegetarian "bacon"

1 cup shredded Cheddar cheese or vegan Cheddar

1 teaspoon salt

¼ teaspoon black pepper

Add all ingredients to a 4-quart slow cooker, cover, and cook on medium-high heat for 4–5 hours.

PER SERVING Calories: 504 | Fat: 25 g | Protein: 18 g | Sodium: 1,348 mg | Fiber: 8 g | Carbohydrates: 64 g | Sugar: 9 g

Potato Risotto

Finely diced potato replaces arborio rice in this spin on a classic. You can replace the spinach with peas if you like.

INGREDIENTS | SERVES 4

2 leeks (white part only)

¼ cup olive oil

3 sprigs fresh thyme, chopped

3 pounds russet potatoes, peeled and finely diced

2 cups dry white wine

5 cups Vegetable Broth (see Chapter 3)

1 teaspoon salt

¼ teaspoon black pepper

4 cups fresh spinach

1. Thinly slice the leeks crosswise into semicircles and rinse.

2. Add the olive oil to a 4-quart slow cooker and sauté the leeks on high heat until translucent, about 5–7 minutes.

3. Add the rest of the ingredients except for the spinach. Cover and cook on medium-high heat for 4 hours.

4. Mix the spinach into the risotto and continue cooking for 1 more hour.

PER SERVING Calories: 580 | Fat: 12 g | Protein: 10 g | Sodium: 741 mg | Fiber: 7 g | Carbohydrates: 74 g | Sugar: 9 g

Scalloped Potatoes

*These easy scalloped potatoes go well with a piece of
mock meatloaf and a heaping scoop of green beans.*

INGREDIENTS | SERVES 8

½ white onion, julienned

2 cloves garlic, minced

3 cups Vegan Alfredo sauce (see Chapter 6)

1 teaspoon salt

¼ teaspoon black pepper

½ cup water

4 potatoes, thinly sliced

1 teaspoon salt

¼ teaspoon black pepper

Add all ingredients to a 4-quart slow cooker. Cover and cook on medium-high heat for 4 hours.

PER SERVING Calories: 302 | Fat: 15 g | Protein: 8 g | Sodium: 1,214 mg | Fiber: 3 g | Carbohydrates: 33 g | Sugar: 4 g

Choosing Onions

Choosing the right type of onion is important for the outcome of your dish because each has a distinct flavor. Yellow onions are a little sweeter, especially Vidalia onions. White onions should be used in dishes like this, where you don't want the flavor to stand out.

Potatoes Au Gratin

For rich dishes high in fat, serve a smaller portion and balance it with a healthy veggie on the side.

INGREDIENTS | SERVES 8

½ cup water

8 cups potatoes, peeled and diced

2 cups Vegan Alfredo sauce (see Chapter 6)

1 cup shredded Cheddar cheese or vegan Cheddar

1 teaspoon salt

¼ teaspoon black pepper

Add all ingredients to a 4-quart slow cooker. Cover and cook on medium-high heat for 4 hours.

PER SERVING Calories: 311 | Fat: 15 g | Protein: 10 g | Sodium: 1,117 mg | Fiber: 4 g | Carbohydrates: 34 g | Sugar: 3 g

Rosemary Fingerling Potatoes

Fingerling potatoes are small, long potatoes that look a little like fingers.

INGREDIENTS | SERVES 6

2 tablespoons extra-virgin olive oil

1½ pounds fingerling potatoes

1 teaspoon salt

¼ teaspoon black pepper

2 tablespoons fresh rosemary, chopped

1 tablespoon fresh lemon juice

Time Saver

To save on time when cooking potatoes, always cut them into the smallest pieces the recipe will allow and cook at the highest temperature. For this recipe, you can quarter the potatoes and cook on high heat.

1. Add the olive oil, potatoes, salt, and pepper to a 4-quart slow cooker. Cover and cook on low heat for 3–4 hours.

2. Remove the cover and mix in the rosemary and lemon juice.

PER SERVING Calories: 121 | Fat: 5 g | Protein: 2 g | Sodium: 401 mg | Fiber: 3.2 g | Carbohydrates: 18.5 g | Sugar: 1 g

Dill Red Potatoes

Fresh dill is the perfect herb to season a summer dish.

INGREDIENTS | SERVES 6

2 tablespoons extra-virgin olive oil

1½ pounds red potatoes

1 teaspoon salt

¼ teaspoon black pepper

2 tablespoons fresh dill, chopped

½ teaspoon lemon pepper

1. Add the olive oil, potatoes, salt, and pepper to a 4-quart slow cooker. Cover, and cook on low heat for 3–4 hours.

2. Remove the cover and mix in the dill and lemon pepper.

PER SERVING Calories: 118 | Fat: 4.6 g | Protein: 2 g | Sodium: 400 mg | Fiber: 2 g | Carbohydrates: 18 g | Sugar: 1 g

Chipotle and Thyme Sweet Potatoes

To substitute fresh thyme for dried thyme, use ½ tablespoon of the fresh herb.

INGREDIENTS | SERVES 6

6 cups sweet potatoes, cubed
4 tablespoons butter or vegan margarine
3 cloves garlic, minced
1 teaspoon dried chipotle pepper
½ teaspoon dried thyme
1 teaspoon salt
¼ teaspoon black pepper

Add all ingredients to a 4-quart slow cooker. Cover and cook on medium heat for 4 hours.

PER SERVING Calories: 185 | Fat: 8 g | Protein: 2 g | Sodium: 468 mg | Fiber: 4 g | Carbohydrates: 28 g | Sugar: 5.6 g

Maple-Glazed Sweet Potatoes

You can reduce the amount of sugar in this recipe by choosing a no-sugar-added syrup.

INGREDIENTS | SERVES 4

4 cups sweet potatoes, cubed
2 tablespoons butter or vegan margarine
¼ cup maple syrup
⅓ cup chopped pecans

Add all ingredients to a 4-quart slow cooker. Cover and cook on medium heat for 4 hours.

PER SERVING Calories: 280 | Fat: 12 g | Protein: 3 g | Sodium: 76 mg | Fiber: 5 g | Carbohydrates: 42 g | Sugar: 18 g

Recipe Substitutions

It's okay to use inexpensive pancake syrup instead of pure maple syrup in this recipe. It won't be as flavorful as pure maple syrup, but it will do the job.

Herbed Potatoes

Any combination of herbs will work in this potato dish.
Rosemary, thyme, dill, and coriander are great alternatives.

INGREDIENTS | SERVES 4

2 tablespoons olive oil

1 onion, diced

8 cups red potatoes, quartered

1 teaspoon dried oregano

1 teaspoon dried basil

1 teaspoon salt

¼ teaspoon black pepper

1. Add the olive oil to a 4-quart slow cooker and sauté the onion on high heat until translucent, about 3–5 minutes.

2. Add the remaining ingredients to the slow cooker. Cover, and cook on medium heat for 4 hours.

PER SERVING Calories: 232 | Fat: 7 g | Protein: 5 g | Sodium: 609 mg | Fiber: 5 g | Carbohydrates: 50 g | Sugar: 4 g

Potato Piccata

Piccata typically means a dish that contains butter, lemon, and herbs.
Italian parsley, capers, garlic, and shallots are also commonly used.

INGREDIENTS | SERVES 4

2 tablespoons butter or vegan margarine

1 onion, julienned

1 red pepper, sliced

4 russet potatoes, sliced

¼ cup Vegetable Broth (see Chapter 3)

2 tablespoons fresh lemon juice

1 teaspoon salt

¼ teaspoon black pepper

¼ cup parsley, chopped

1. Add the butter or margarine to a 2-quart slow cooker and sauté the onions and peppers on high heat until they are golden brown, about 5–7 minutes.

2. Add the rest of the ingredients except for the parsley. Cover and cook on medium heat for 4 hours. Mix in the parsley.

PER SERVING Calories: 218 | Fat: 6 g | Protein: 5 g | Sodium: 611 mg | Fiber: 4 g | Carbohydrates: 44 g | Sugar: 4 g

Sweet Potato Salad

This salad, like many others, can be served warm and straight out of the slow cooker or chilled before serving.

INGREDIENTS | SERVES 6

3 tablespoons extra-virgin olive oil

1 onion, chopped

3 cloves garlic, minced

1 pound sweet potatoes, peeled and cubed

½ teaspoon dried ginger

½ teaspoon paprika

1 teaspoon cumin

1 teaspoon salt

¼ teaspoon black pepper

1 tablespoon fresh lemon juice

¼ cup fresh parsley, chopped

1. Add the olive oil to the slow cooker and saute the onions and garlic on high heat until they are golden brown, about 2–3 minutes.

2. Add the rest of the ingredients except for the lemon juice and parsley. Cover and cook on medium heat for 4 hours.

3. Mix the lemon juice and parsley into the sweet potato salad.

PER SERVING Calories: 158 | Fat: 7 g | Protein: 2 g | Sodium: 438 mg | Fiber: 3 g | Carbohydrates: 18 g | Sugar: 4 g

Potato Peels

For most recipes, it's the cook's personal preference whether or not to leave the skins on or peel them. Although in this recipe either way works fine, consider leaving them on—the 2 grams of fiber per serving contained in the skin equals or exceeds the amount in many whole-grain foods.

Mexican Spice Potatoes

If you like things spicy, really kick it up by adding an extra teaspoon of cayenne to these potatoes!

INGREDIENTS | SERVES 4

6 cups red potatoes, cubed
1 teaspoon chili powder
½ teaspoon sugar
½ teaspoon paprika
⅛ teaspoon cayenne pepper
⅛ teaspoon garlic powder
¼ teaspoon cumin
½ teaspoon salt
⅛ teaspoon black pepper
½ cup water

Add all ingredients to a 4-quart slow cooker. Cover and cook on medium heat for 4 hours.

PER SERVING Calories: 163 | Fat: 0 g | Protein: 4 g | Sodium: 316 mg | Fiber: 4 g | Carbohydrates: 37 g | Sugar: 3 g

Garlic-Parmesan Mashed Potatoes

Red potatoes break down easily, but become creamy, not crumbly, when mashed.

INGREDIENTS | SERVES 8

½ cup butter or vegan margarine
6 cloves garlic, minced
1½ pounds red potatoes, quartered
2 cups unsweetened soymilk
1 cup Parmesan cheese or vegan Parmesan
1 teaspoon salt
¼ teaspoon black pepper
¼ cup fresh parsley, chopped

1. Add the butter or vegan margarine to the slow cooker and sauté the garlic on high heat until it is golden brown, about 1 minute.

2. Add the rest of the ingredients except for the parsley. Cover and cook on medium heat for 4 hours.

3. Mix in the parsley and mash the potatoes to the desired consistency.

PER SERVING Calories: 252 | Fat: 16 g | Protein: 9 g | Sodium: 558 mg | Fiber: 2 g | Carbohydrates: 19 g | Sugar: 3 g

Vegan Parmesan

Vegan Parmesan cheese is easy to find online and is available at stores around the country. If you can't find it at a store near you, try ordering Parma! Vegan Parmesan from CosmosVeganShoppe.com.

Potato-Broccoli Casserole

For a lighter and thinner sauce, use milk or unsweetened soymilk instead of Vegan Alfredo sauce.

INGREDIENTS | SERVES 8

1½ pounds red potatoes

2 cups broccoli florets

3 cups Vegan Alfredo sauce (see Chapter 6)

1 teaspoon lemon pepper

½ teaspoon red pepper flakes

½ teaspoon garlic powder

1 teaspoon salt

¼ teaspoon black pepper

Add all ingredients to a 4-quart slow cooker. Cover and cook on medium heat for 4 hours.

PER SERVING Calories: 292 | Fat: 15 g | Protein: 9 g | Sodium: 1,395 mg | Fiber: 3 g | Carbohydrates: 30 g | Sugar: 3.5 g

Garlic-Parsley Potatoes

The ingredients are similar to mashed potatoes in this dish,
but you enjoy a stronger potato flavor by leaving them in bigger pieces.

INGREDIENTS | SERVES 8

½ cup butter or vegan margarine

6 cloves garlic, minced

1 onion, diced

1½ pounds red potatoes, quartered

½ cup unsweetened soymilk

1 teaspoon salt

¼ teaspoon black pepper

¼ cup parsley

1 tablespoon fresh lemon juice

1. Add the butter or vegan margarine to a 4-quart slow cooker and sauté the garlic and onions on high heat until they are golden brown, about 2–3 minutes.

2. Add the rest of the ingredients except for the parsley and lemon juice. Cover and cook on medium heat for 4 hours.

3. Mix in the parsley and lemon and cook for an additional 30 minutes.

PER SERVING Calories: 173 | Fat: 12 g | Protein: 2 g | Sodium: 311 mg | Fiber: 2 g | Carbohydrates: 15 g | Sugar: 1.5 g

CHAPTER 9

Rice and Grains

Tomatillo Rice

This recipe is similar to jambalaya, in that you cook the rice in a tomato-based sauce so the flavors are completely absorbed.

INGREDIENTS | SERVES 4

2 tablespoons olive oil

½ red onion, diced

½ red bell pepper, diced

2 cloves garlic, minced

Juice of 1 lime

1 cup tomatillo salsa

1 cup water

1 teaspoon salt

1 cup long-grain white rice

½ cup cilantro, chopped

Tomatillos

Tomatillos are small green tomatoes that are used in many Latin-inspired dishes. They come with a papery husk surrounding the edible fruit, which must first be removed. Try to find tomatillos with an intact, tight-fitting, light brown husk; if it is dry or shriveled, the tomatillo is probably not good.

1. Heat the olive oil in a sauté pan over medium heat. Add the onion, bell pepper, and garlic and sauté about 5 minutes.

2. Transfer to a 4-quart slow cooker. Add all the remaining ingredients except for the cilantro.

3. Cover and cook over low heat for 6–8 hours. Check the rice periodically to make sure the liquid hasn't been absorbed too quickly and the rice is not burning.

4. Stir in the cilantro before serving.

PER SERVING Calories: 268 | Fat: 7 g | Protein: 5 g | Sodium: 982 mg | Fiber: 3 g | Carbohydrates: 47 g | Sugar: 3 g

Stuffed Peppers

Try a mixture of green, red, orange, and yellow peppers for this dish.

INGREDIENTS | SERVES 4

4 large bell peppers
½ teaspoon ground chipotle pepper
¼ teaspoon hot Mexican chili powder
¼ teaspoon freshly ground black pepper
⅛ teaspoon salt
1 (15-ounce) can fire-roasted diced tomatoes with garlic
1 cup cooked long-grain rice
1½ cups broccoli florets
¼ cup diced onion
½ cup water

1. Cut the tops off of each pepper to form a cap. Remove the seeds from the cap. Remove the seeds and most of the ribs from inside the pepper.

2. Place the peppers open-side up in a 4- or 6-quart slow cooker.

3. In a medium bowl, mix the spices, tomatoes, rice, broccoli, and onions. Spoon the mixture into each pepper until they are filled to the top. Replace the cap.

4. Pour the water into the bottom of the slow cooker insert. Cook on low for 6 hours.

PER SERVING Calories: 140 | Fat: 0.5 g | Protein: 4 g | Sodium: 480 mg | Fiber: 4 g | Carbohydrates: 28 g | Sugar: 5 g

Vegetable Fried Rice

Sriracha is a popular type of hot sauce that features a rooster on the bottle and is sometimes called "rooster sauce."

INGREDIENTS | SERVES 4

1 tablespoon butter or vegan margarine

2 cups white rice, uncooked

3 garlic cloves, minced

2 cups water

2 cups Vegetable Broth (see Chapter 3)

2½ teaspoons soy sauce

1 teaspoon brown sugar

½ teaspoons Sriracha sauce

1 teaspoon lime juice

1 cup carrots, diced

1 cup broccoli, chopped

1. Rub the butter or margarine around the inside of a 4-quart slow cooker to ensure that the rice will not stick to the edges.

2. Add the rest of the ingredients. Cover and cook on low heat for 4–5 hours.

PER SERVING Calories: 390 | Fat: 3.6 g | Protein: 8 g | Sodium: 258 mg | Fiber: 4 g | Carbohydrates: 70 g | Sugar: 5 g

Adding Eggs

If you eat eggs, you can add a lightly scrambled egg to your rice during the last 30 minutes of the cooking time.

Paella

The spice saffron can be very expensive, but you can use the more affordable turmeric in its place.

INGREDIENTS | SERVES 6

1 tablespoon olive oil
½ onion, diced
1 cup diced tomato
½ teaspoon saffron or turmeric
1 teaspoon salt
2 tablespoons fresh parsley
1 cup long-grain white rice
1 cup frozen peas
2 cups water
1 (12-ounce) package vegan chorizo, crumbled

1. Heat the olive oil in a sauté pan over medium heat. Add the onion and sauté for 3 minutes.

2. Add the tomato, saffron, salt, and parsley and stir.

3. Pour the sautéed mixture into a 4-quart slow cooker. Add the white rice, then frozen peas and water.

4. Cover, and cook on low heat for 4 hours

5. Pour the crumbled chorizo on top of the rice. Cover and cook for an additional 30 minutes. Stir before serving.

PER SERVING Calories: 421 | Fat: 24 g | Protein: 17 g | Sodium: 1,091 mg | Fiber: 2 g | Carbohydrates: 32 g | Sugar: 2.6 g

Eggplant "Lasagna"

This no-noodle dish makes for a hearty vegetarian meal. Serve it with a side salad.

INGREDIENTS | SERVES 8

2 (1-pound) eggplants

1 tablespoon kosher salt

30 ounces skim-milk ricotta or tofu ricotta (see sidebar)

2 teaspoons olive oil, divided use

1 medium onion, diced

3 cloves garlic, minced

1 tablespoon fresh, minced Italian parsley

1 tablespoon fresh, minced basil

28 ounces canned crushed tomatoes

1 shallot, diced

4 ounces fresh spinach

1 tablespoon dried mixed Italian seasoning

¼ teaspoon salt

½ teaspoon freshly ground black pepper

Tofu Ricotta

You can make your own Tofu Ricotta by crumbling one package of drained tofu, then adding 1 tablespoon lemon juice, 1 teaspoon salt, 1 teaspoon dried parsley, and ½ teaspoon pepper.

1. Slice the eggplant lengthwise into ¼"-thick slices. Place in a bowl or colander and sprinkle with the salt. Allow it to sit for 15 minutes. Drain off the liquid. Rinse off the salt. Pat dry. Set aside.

2. Line a colander with cheesecloth or paper towels. Pour the ricotta into the colander and drain for 15 minutes. (If you are using Tofu Ricotta, skip the draining step.)

3. Heat 1 teaspoon olive oil in a nonstick pan. Sauté the onion and garlic until just softened, about 1–2 minutes. Add the parsley, basil, and crushed tomatoes. Sauté until the sauce thickens and the liquid has evaporated, about 20 minutes.

4. In a second nonstick pan, heat the remaining oil. Sauté the shallot and spinach until the spinach has wilted, about 30 seconds to 1 minute. Drain off any extra liquid.

5. Stir the shallot-spinach mixture, Italian seasoning, salt, and pepper into the ricotta mixture. Set aside.

6. Preheat the oven to 375°F. Place the eggplant slices on baking sheets. Bake for 10 minutes. Cool slightly.

7. Pour ⅓ of the sauce onto the bottom of a 4-quart slow cooker. Top with a single layer of eggplant. Top with ½ of the cheese mixture. Add ⅓ of the sauce. Top with the rest of the cheese mixture.

8. Layer the remaining eggplant on top, then top with remaining sauce. Cover, and cook for 4 hours on low, then uncovered 30 minutes on high.

PER SERVING Calories: 240 | Fat: 10 g | Protein: 16 g | Sodium: 1,250 mg | Fiber: 5 g | Carbohydrates: 20 g | Sugar: 3 g

Portobello Barley

This method of cooking barley makes it as creamy as risotto, but with the bonus of being high in fiber.

INGREDIENTS | SERVES 8

1 teaspoon olive oil

2 shallots, minced

2 cloves garlic, minced

3 portobello mushroom caps, sliced

1 cup pearl barley

3¼ cups water

¼ teaspoon salt

½ teaspoon freshly ground black pepper

1 teaspoon crushed rosemary

1 teaspoon dried chervil

¼ cup grated Parmesan or vegan Parmesan

Chervil

Chervil is an herb of the parsley family. It has delicate, curly leaves almost like carrot tops. Its mild flavor, which includes hints of anise, is easily overwhelmed by stronger flavors. Fresh parsley, tarragon, or a combination of both can easily substitute for chervil.

1. Heat the oil in a nonstick skillet. Sauté the shallots, garlic, and mushrooms until softened, about 3–4 minutes.

2. Place the mushroom mixture into a 4-quart slow cooker. Add the barley, water, salt, pepper, rosemary, and chervil. Stir.

3. Cover, and cook on low for 8–9 hours or on high for 4 hours.

4. Turn off the slow cooker and stir in the Parmesan. Serve immediately.

PER SERVING Calories: 130 | Fat: 1.5 g | Protein: 5 g | Sodium: 120 mg | Fiber: 5 g | Carbohydrates: 25 g | Sugar: 1 g

Wild Mushroom Risotto

This makes a great side dish, but you can also try it as a main course, paired with a green salad.

INGREDIENTS | SERVES 6

1 teaspoon olive oil

1 shallot, minced

2 cloves garlic, minced

8 ounces sliced assorted wild mushrooms

2 cups Vegetable Broth (see Chapter 3)

2 cups arborio rice

3 cups water

½ teaspoon salt

1. Heat the oil in a nonstick pan. Sauté the shallot, garlic, and mushrooms until soft, about 4–5 minutes.

2. Add ½ cup broth and the rice and cook until the liquid is fully absorbed, about 5 minutes.

3. Scrape the rice mixture into a 4-quart slow cooker. Add the water, salt, and remaining broth.

4. Cover and cook on low for 1 hour. Stir before serving.

PER SERVING Calories: 272 | Fat: 1.2 g | Protein: 6 g | Sodium: 228 mg | Fiber: 3 g | Carbohydrates: 58 g | Sugar: 2.7 g

Wild Rice with Mixed Vegetables

Wild rice cooks up perfectly in the slow cooker. Try it as a high-fiber alternative to white rice or potatoes.

INGREDIENTS | SERVES 8

2½ cups water

1 cup wild rice

3 cloves garlic, minced

1 medium onion, diced

1 carrot, diced

1 stalk celery, diced

Wild, Wild Rice

Wild rice is a bit of a misnomer. It is actually a North American grass that grows in shallow water, predominantly in the Great Lakes region. It is high in protein and carbohydrates and very low in fat. While it is often sold in mixes with white rice, it is also tasty all by itself.

1. Place all ingredients into a 4-quart slow cooker and stir. Cover and cook on low for 4 hours.

2. After 4 hours, check to see if the kernels are open and tender. If not, put the lid back on and continue to cook for an additional 15–30 minutes.

3. Stir before serving.

PER SERVING Calories: 90 | Fat: 0 g | Protein: 3 g | Sodium: 15 mg | Fiber: 2 g | Carbohydrates: 18 g | Sugar: 2 g

Saffron Rice

Better Than Bouillon makes a delicious No Chicken base that can be used to make stock.

INGREDIENTS | SERVES 4

2 cups white rice, uncooked

2 tablespoons margarine

2 cups water

2 cups vegetarian chicken stock

¾ teaspoons saffron threads

1 teaspoon salt

1. Add all ingredients to a 4-quart slow cooker. Cover and cook on low heat for 4–5 hours.

2. Check the rice to see if it is tender. If not, cook for another 30–45 minutes.

PER SERVING Calories: 420 | Fat: 7 g | Protein: 9 g | Sodium: 882 mg | Fiber: 1.5 g | Carbohydrates: 82 g | Sugar: 2 g

Bulgur with Broccoli and Carrot

This filling and delicious dish makes a comforting meal on a cold day.
Make it complete with a salad or a light soup from Chapter 3.

INGREDIENTS | SERVES 4

2 cups bulgur, uncooked

2 tablespoons butter or vegan margarine

1 cup carrots, diced

1 cup broccoli, chopped

2 cups Vegetable Broth (see Chapter 3)

1 teaspoon salt

1. Add all ingredients to a 4-quart slow cooker. Cover and cook on low heat for 6 hours.

2. Check the rice to see if it is tender and if not, cook for 1 more hour.

PER SERVING Calories: 360 | Fat: 6 g | Protein: 9 g | Sodium: 656 mg | Fiber: 10 g | Carbohydrates: 13 g | Sugar: 4.6 g

Bulgur, the World's Oldest Cooked Cereal

Bulgur was being eaten as a warm cooked cereal by Early Neolithic Bulgarians from between 5920 B.C. to 5730 B.C. It is a type of whole-wheat grain that has been cleaned, parboiled, dried, ground into particles, and sifted into size. It is high in fiber, B vitamins, iron, phosphorous, and manganese. Its pleasant nutty flavor makes it not just healthy but delicious, too.

Red Beans and Rice

Red beans and rice is a classic New Orleans dish that can be cooked with the rice and beans mixed together.

INGREDIENTS | SERVES 4

3 cups water

3½ cups vegetarian chicken stock

2 tablespoons butter or vegan margarine

1 (15-ounce) can kidney beans, drained

2 cups white rice, uncooked

1 onion, chopped

1 green bell pepper, chopped

1 cup celery, chopped

1 teaspoon thyme

1 teaspoon paprika

1 teaspoon Cajun seasoning

½ teaspoon red pepper flakes

1 teaspoon salt

¼ teaspoons black pepper

1. Add all ingredients to a 4-quart slow cooker. Cover and cook on low heat for 6 hours.

2. Check the rice to see if it is tender and if not, cook for an additional hour.

PER SERVING Calories: 340 | Fat: 7 g | Protein: 11 g | Sodium: 887 mg | Fiber: 8 g | Carbohydrates: 52 g | Sugar: 4.5 g

Recipe Variations

For a heartier meal, add sliced vegetarian sausage or vegetarian beef crumbles during the last hour of cooking.

Mock Chicken and Rice

Brown rice, white rice, or wild rice will all work in this recipe.

INGREDIENTS | SERVES 8

2 tablespoons olive oil

1 cup mushrooms, sliced

½ cup onions, sliced

2 cups white rice, uncooked

2 tablespoons butter or vegan margarine

2 cups water

2 cups vegetarian chicken broth

2 (7-ounce) packages Gardein Chick'n Strips

½ teaspoon salt

⅛ teaspoon black pepper

1. Add the olive oil to a 4-quart slow cooker and sauté the mushrooms and onions on high heat until browned, about 3–5 minutes.

2. Add the rest of the ingredients to the slow cooker. Cover and cook on low heat for 6 hours.

PER SERVING Calories: 310 | Fat: 8 g | Protein: 11 g | Sodium: 523 mg | Fiber: 1 g | Carbohydrates: 42 g | Sugar: 0.6 g

Spanish Rice

Cooking rice in tomatoes, chili powder, and bell pepper is the key to Spanish rice.

INGREDIENTS | SERVES 8

2 cups white rice, uncooked

2 tablespoons butter or vegan margarine

2 cups water

2 cups Vegetable Broth (see Chapter 3)

1 onion, diced

1 green bell pepper, diced

1 cup canned tomatoes, diced

⅛ cup pickled jalapeños, diced

1 teaspoon chili powder

½ teaspoon garlic powder

1 teaspoon salt

¼ teaspoon black pepper

Add all ingredients to a 4-quart slow cooker. Cover and cook on low heat for 4–5 hours.

PER SERVING Calories: 230 | Fat: 3 g | Protein: 4 g | Sodium: 399 mg | Fiber: 2.5 g | Carbohydrates: 45 g | Sugar: 3 g

Brown Rice and Vegetables

This recipe is simple, easy, and healthy. Yum!

INGREDIENTS | SERVES 8

2 cups brown rice, uncooked
2 tablespoons butter or vegan margarine
3 cups Vegetable Broth (see Chapter 3)
2 cups water
½ cup yellow squash, chopped
½ cup zucchini, chopped
½ onion, chopped
½ cup button mushrooms, sliced
½ cup red bell pepper, chopped
1 teaspoon salt
¼ teaspoon black pepper

Add all ingredients to a 4-quart slow cooker. Cover and cook on low heat for 4–5 hours.

PER SERVING Calories: 225 | Fat: 4 g | Protein: 4.6 g | Sodium: 329 mg | Fiber: 3 g | Carbohydrates: 42 g | Sugar: 3 g

Curried Rice

Curried rice is a great side for Palak Tofu (See Chapter 11).

INGREDIENTS | SERVES 4

2 cups white rice, uncooked
2 tablespoons olive oil
2 cups water
2 cups No-Beef Broth (see Chapter 3)
2 tablespoons curry powder
1 teaspoons salt
¼ teaspoons black pepper
1 tablespoon lime juice
¼ cup cilantro, chopped

1. Add all the ingredients to a 4-quart slow cooker except the lime juice and cilantro.

2. Cover and cook on low heat for 4–5 hours.

3. Stir in the lime juice and cilantro and cook for 30 more minutes before serving.

PER SERVING Calories: 387 | Fat: 1 g | Protein: 7.6 g | Sodium: 634 mg | Fiber: 4 g | Carbohydrates: 85 g | Sugar: 3 g

CHAPTER 10

Beans

Chipotle Black Bean Salad

There are actually 5 different varieties of black beans, but when you purchase bolack beans, they are often just labeled as black beans.

INGREDIENTS | SERVES 8

1 (16-ounce) bag dried black beans
Enough water to cover beans by 1"
2 teaspoons salt
1 tablespoon chipotle powder
2 teaspoons thyme
2 fresh tomatoes, diced
1 red onion, diced
¼ cup cilantro, chopped

1. Add black beans, water, and salt to a 4-quart slow cooker. Cover and cook on medium heat for about 5–6 hours. Check the beans at about 5 hours and continue cooking if necessary.

2. Once the beans are done, drain in a colander and allow to cool to room temperature.

3. Mix in the remaining ingredients and serve.

PER SERVING Calories: 198 | Fat: 1 g | Protein: 10 g | Sodium: 768 mg | Fiber: 7 g | Carbohydrates: 37 g | Sugar: 2.5 g

Prepping Dried Beans

Before cooking with dried beans, you must first rinse the beans, soak them overnight in a pot full of water, and then boil them for 10 minutes. They are then ready for Step 1 of the recipe.

Mediterranean Chickpeas

Chickpeas, also known as garbanzo beans, are the main ingredient in this delicious dish that can be served hot or cold.

INGREDIENTS | SERVES 8

2 (15-ounce) cans chickpeas, drained
1 cup water
4 teaspoons salt
¼ cup extra-virgin olive oil
1 teaspoon black pepper
1 cup fresh basil, chopped
5 cloves garlic, minced
2 tomatoes, diced
½ cup kalamata olives, sliced

Add all ingredients to a 4-quart slow cooker. Cover and cook on low heat for 4 hours.

PER SERVING Calories: 243 | Fat: 8 g | Protein: 7 g | Sodium: 1,208 mg | Fiber: 6 g | Carbohydrates: 37 g | Sugar: 3 g

Open-Faced Bean Burrito

Salsas come in many different flavors depending on which ingredients are used but any type of salsa (except fruit based salsa) will work in this recipe.

INGREDIENTS | SERVES 8

1 (16-ounce) bag dried black beans

Water, enough to cover beans by 1"

4 teaspoons salt

1 tablespoon chili powder

2 teaspoons cumin

2 teaspoons garlic powder

1 teaspoon black pepper

1 (15-ounce) can corn, drained

2 fresh tomatoes, diced

8 large flour tortillas

4 cups cooked brown rice

2 cups shredded Cheddar cheese or vegan Cheddar cheese

2 cups salsa

¼ cup cilantro, chopped

Alternate Suggestions

Burrito fillings can easily be used in other dishes. Try the beans, rice and toppings over a bed of lettuce for a taco salad, in soft corn tortillas for delicious tacos or as a hearty meal on their own.

1. Rinse the black beans, then soak overnight. Drain the water, rinse again, then add to a large pot and cover with water. Boil on high heat for 10 minutes, then drain.

2. Add black beans, water, and 2 teaspoons of salt to a 4-quart slow cooker. Cover and cook on medium heat for about 5–6 hours. Check the beans at about 5 hours to see if they are fork-tender and continue cooking if necessary.

3. Once the beans are done, drain in a colander and allow to cool to room temperature. Then, in a large bowl, mix in the remaining salt, chili powder, cumin, garlic powder, black pepper, corn, and tomatoes.

4. Place a tortilla on a plate, add a scoop of the brown rice and then a scoop of the black bean mixture. Top with the cheese, salsa, and cilantro, if desired.

PER SERVING Calories: 798 | Fat: 18 g | Protein: 27 g | Sodium: 2,629 mg | Fiber: 12 g | Carbohydrates: 120 g | Sugar: 6 g

Refried Beans

Refried beans can be made with black beans or the more commonly used pinto beans. Serve it as a side dish at your next Mexican meal.

INGREDIENTS | SERVES 8

1 (16-ounce) bag dried pinto beans
Enough water to cover beans by 1"
4 teaspoons salt
¼ cup olive oil
6 cloves garlic, minced
1 teaspoon black pepper

1. Rinse the pinto beans, then soak overnight. Drain the water, rinse again.

2. In a large pot, add the beans and cover with water. Boil on high heat for 10 minutes, then drain.

3. Add pinto beans, water, salt, olive oil, and garlic to a 4-quart slow cooker. Cover and cook on medium heat for about 5–6 hours. Check the beans at about 5 hours and continue cooking if necessary.

4. Once the beans are done, drain in a colander. Add the black pepper and mash the beans with a potato masher or the back side of a wooden spoon. Add water, if necessary, to create the desired consistency.

PER SERVING Calories: 232 | Fat: 7 g | Protein: 9 g | Sodium: 1,186 mg | Fiber: 7 g | Carbohydrates: 32 g | Sugar: 1 g

Cuban Black Beans

Traditionally served with rice, Cuban-style black beans are also great served with tortillas and fresh avocado slices.

INGREDIENTS | SERVES 4

½ teaspoon apple cider vinegar

¼ cup diced onion

1 (15-ounce) canned black beans, drained

2 cloves garlic, minced

1 jalapeño, minced

½ teaspoon oregano

¼ teaspoon cumin

1. Place all ingredients into a 2-quart slow cooker. Stir to distribute all the ingredients evenly.

2. Cover and cook on low for 6–8 hours. Stir before serving.

PER SERVING Calories: 80 | Fat: 1 g | Protein: 6 g | Sodium: 530 mg | Fiber: 6 g | Carbohydrates: 19 g | Sugar: 2.5 g

Cuban Cuisine

Cuban cuisine is influenced by French, African, Arab, Chinese, Portuguese, and Spanish cultures. Traditionally primarily a peasant food, it is rarely fried but rather sautéed or slow cooked, and is unconcerned with exact measurements. Many dishes have a sofrito for their base, a mixture of onion, green pepper, garlic, oregano, and ground pepper quick-fried in olive oil, used to cook black beans as well as other dishes.

Curried Lentils

Serve this Indian-style dish with hot rice or naan, an Indian flat bread.
It can also be served with plain yogurt or vegan yogurt as garnish or on the side.

INGREDIENTS | SERVES 6

2 teaspoons butter or canola oil
1 large onion, thinly sliced
2 cloves garlic, minced
2 jalapeños, diced
½ teaspoon red pepper flakes
½ teaspoon ground cumin
1 pound yellow lentils
6 cups water
½ teaspoon salt
½ teaspoon ground turmeric
4 cups chopped fresh spinach

1. Heat the butter or oil in a nonstick pan. Sauté the onion slices until they start to brown, about 8–10 minutes.

2. Add the garlic, jalapeños, red pepper flakes, and cumin. Sauté for 2–3 minutes.

3. Add the onion mixture to a 4-quart slow cooker.

4. Sort through the lentils and discard any rocks or foreign matter. Add the lentils to the slow cooker. Stir in the water, salt, and turmeric.

5. Cover and cook on high for 2½ hours.

6. Add the spinach and stir. Cook on high for an additional 15 minutes.

PER SERVING Calories: 280 | Fat: 2 g | Protein: 21 g | Sodium: 210 mg | Fiber: 10 g | Carbohydrates: 49 g | Sugar: 2.5 g

Hoppin' John

Hoppin' John is traditionally eaten on New Year's Day. Eating it as the first meal of the day is supposed to ensure health and prosperity for the coming year.

INGREDIENTS | SERVES 8

1 cup dried black-eyed peas, rehydrated
¾ cup water
1 teaspoon liquid smoke
1 teaspoon red pepper flakes
3 cups diced mustard or collard greens
14 ounces canned tomatoes
½ teaspoon freshly ground black pepper
¼ teaspoon salt
1 teaspoon dried oregano

1. Place all ingredients into a 4-quart slow cooker. Stir.

2. Cover and cook on high for 5 hours.

PER SERVING Calories: 80 g | Fat: 0.5 g | Protein: 5 g | Sodium: 220 mg | Fiber: 6 g | Carbohydrates: 12 g | Sugar: 2.5 g

Quick Prep for Black-Eyed Peas

Here's a method to quickly and easily prepare black-eyed peas. Place the peas in a large stockpot. Cover completely with water, and bring to a boil. Boil 2 minutes, reduce heat, and simmer for 1 hour.

Bourbon Baked Beans

Serve these at your next cookout or as a side dish for BBQ tempeh or tofu.

INGREDIENTS | SERVES 8

1 large sweet onion, peeled and diced

3 (15-ounce) cans cannellini, great northern, or navy beans

1 (15-ounce) can diced tomatoes

¼ cup maple syrup

3 tablespoons apple cider vinegar

1 teaspoon liquid smoke

4 cloves garlic, peeled and minced

2 tablespoons dry mustard

1½ teaspoons freshly ground black pepper

½ teaspoon ground ginger

¼ teaspoon dried red pepper flakes

2 tablespoons bourbon

Salt, to taste

1. Add all ingredients to a 4-quart slow cooker. Stir until combined.

2. Cover and cook on low heat for 6 hours. Taste for seasoning and add additional salt, if needed.

PER SERVING Calories: 290 | Fat: 2 g | Protein: 15 g | Sodium: 130 mg | Fiber: 9 g | Carbohydrates: 48 g | Sugar: 9 g

Recipe Variations

Some Bourbon Baked Beans recipes include much more tomato than this one. If you prefer more tomato, you can add 1 (4-ounce) can of tomato paste or about 2 tablespoons of ketchup when you stir in all of the other ingredients.

Pinto Beans

Try mashing pinto beans with a little vegetable broth to make vegetarian refried beans.

INGREDIENTS | SERVES 8

1 (16-ounce) bag dried pinto beans
Enough water to cover beans by 1"
2 teaspoons salt

1. Rinse the pinto beans, then soak overnight. Drain the water and rinse the beans again.

2. In a large pot, add beans and cover them with water. Boil on high heat for 10 minutes, then drain.

3. Add pinto beans, water, and salt to a 4-quart slow cooker. Cover and cook on medium heat for about 5–6 hours. Check the beans at about 5 hours and continue cooking if necessary.

4. Once the beans are done, drain in a colander.

PER SERVING Calories: 194 | Fat: 0.7 g | Protein: 12 g | Sodium: 597 mg | Fiber: 6 g | Carbohydrates: 35 g | Sugar: 1 g

Adzuki Beans

Adzuki beans are an Asian bean typically enjoyed sweetened, but they are good served savory, too.

INGREDIENTS | SERVES 8

1 (16-ounce) bag dried adzuki beans
Enough water to cover beans by 1"
2 teaspoons salt

1. Rinse the adzuki beans, then soak overnight. Drain the water and rinse the beans again.

2. In a large pot, add beans and cover with water. Boil on high heat for 10 minutes, then drain.

3. Add adzuki beans, water, and salt to a 4-quart slow cooker. Cover and cook on medium heat for about 5–6 hours. Check the beans at about 5 hours and continue cooking if necessary.

4. Once the beans are done, drain in a colander.

PER SERVING Calories: 184 | Fat: 0.3 g | Protein: 11 g | Sodium: 593 mg | Fiber: 7 g | Carbohydrates: 35 g | Sugar: 0 g

Lima Beans and Dumplings

Dumplings can be added to just about any dish that has a fair amount of liquid in it to create a home-style flavor.

INGREDIENTS | SERVES 8

1 (16-ounce) bag dried lima beans

Enough water to cover beans by 1"

2 teaspoons salt

1 (10-ounce) package vegan refrigerated biscuit dough

Vegan Biscuit Dough

You can make vegan biscuit dough by using Bisquick mix and substituting vegan ingredients, or you can purchase an "accidentally vegan" refrigerated dough in your grocery store.

1. Rinse the lima beans, then soak overnight. Drain the water and then rinse the beans again.

2. In a large pot, add the beans and cover with water. Boil on high heat for 10 minutes, then drain.

3. Add lima beans, water, and salt to a 4-quart slow cooker. Cover and cook on medium heat for about 5–6 hours. Check the beans at about 5 hours and continue cooking if necessary.

4. While the beans cook, roll out the biscuit dough, then tear each biscuit into fourths.

5. Once the beans are nearly done, drop in the biscuit pieces, cover, and cook for an additional 30 minutes.

PER SERVING Calories: 281 | Fat: 3 g | Protein: 14 g | Sodium: 834 mg | Fiber: 10 g | Carbohydrates: 52 g | Sugar: 5 g

Black Beans

*Black beans are a versatile ingredient, and you can kick up the flavor
by adding dried chili powder to them while cooking.*

INGREDIENTS | SERVES 8

1 (16-ounce) bag dried black beans

Enough water to cover beans by 1"

2 teaspoons salt

1. Rinse the black beans, then soak overnight. Drain the water and rinse the beans again.

2. In a large pot, add the beans and cover with water. Boil on high heat for 10 minutes, then drain.

3. Add black beans, water, and salt to a 4-quart slow cooker. Cover and cook on medium heat for about 5–6 hours. Check the beans at about 5 hours to see if they are fork-tender and continue cooking if necessary.

4. Once the beans are done, drain in a colander.

PER SERVING Calories: 191 | Fat: 0.8 g | Protein: 12 g | Sodium: 589 mg | Fiber: 8 g | Carbohydrates: 35 g | Sugar: 1.2 g

White Beans

Adding a little salt while cooking will help bring out the flavor of the beans, but this ingredient is optional.

INGREDIENTS | SERVES 8

1 (16-ounce) bag dried white beans
Enough water to cover beans by 1"
2 teaspoons salt
2 bay leaves

The Bay Leaf

Bay leaves are often used to season soups and stews, but before adding them it's best to crumble the leaf in order to extract the most flavor. If you choose to crumble them, it's best to place them in an herb bag or cheesecloth so that you can easily remove them after cooking.

1. Rinse the white beans, then soak overnight. Drain the water and rinse the beans again.

2. In a large pot, add the beans and cover with water. Boil on high heat for 10 minutes, then drain.

3. Add white beans, water, salt, and bay leaves to a 4-quart slow cooker. Cover and cook on medium heat for about 5–6 hours. Check the beans at about 5 hours and continue cooking if necessary.

4. Once the beans are done, drain in a colander and remove the bay leaves.

PER SERVING Calories: 189 | Fat: 0.4 g | Protein: 12 g | Sodium: 600 mg | Fiber: 8 g | Carbohydrates: 35.5 g | Sugar: 4.8 g

Black-Eyed Peas

Beans can be stored in the freezer for several months as long as they are sealed in an airtight bag.

INGREDIENTS | SERVES 8

1 (16-ounce) bag dried black-eyed peas

Enough water to cover black-eyed peas by 1"

2 teaspoons salt

1 teaspoon liquid smoke

1. Rinse the black-eyed peas, then soak overnight. Drain the water and then rinse the peas again.

2. Add the peas to a large pot and cover with water. Boil on high heat for 10 minutes, then drain.

3. Add black-eyed peas, water, salt, and liquid smoke to a 4-quart slow cooker. Cover and cook on medium heat for about 5–6 hours. Check the black-eyed peas at about 5 hours and continue cooking if necessary.

4. Once the black-eyed peas are done, drain in a colander.

PER SERVING Calories: 188 | Fat: 0.7 g | Protein: 13 g | Sodium: 599 mg | Fiber: 6 g | Carbohydrates: 33 g | Sugar: 4 g

Lentils

Lentils are commonly used in Indian cuisine and are delicious with curry paste mixed in.

INGREDIENTS | SERVES 8

1 (16-ounce) bag dried lentils

Enough water to cover lentils by 1"

2 teaspoons salt

1. Add lentils, water, and salt to a 4-quart slow cooker. Cover and cook on medium heat for about 3–4 hours. Check the lentils at about 5 hours and continue cooking if necessary.

2. Once the lentils are done, drain in a colander.

PER SERVING Calories: 198 | Fat: 0.6 g | Protein: 14 g | Sodium: 583 mg | Fiber: 6 g | Carbohydrates: 33 g | Sugar: 1 g

Mexican Beer Black Beans

Try a Mexican beer such as Negra Modelo, Tecate, or Corona to complement the beans in this recipe.

INGREDIENTS | SERVES 8

1 (16-ounce) bag dried black beans
Enough water to cover beans by ½"
2 (12-ounce) bottles light-colored beer
4 teaspoons salt
1 red onion, diced
4 cloves garlic, minced
2 fresh tomatoes, diced
½ cup cilantro, chopped
1 lime, juiced

1. Rinse the black beans, then soak overnight. Drain the water and then rinse the beans again.

2. Add the beans to a large pot and cover with water. Boil on high heat for 10 minutes, then drain.

3. Add black beans, water, beer, and 2 teaspoons salt to a 4-quart slow cooker. Cover and cook on medium heat for about 5–6 hours. Check the beans at about 5 hours and continue cooking if necessary.

4. Once the beans are done, drain in a colander.

5. In a large bowl, combine the beans, remaining salt, red onions, garlic, tomatoes, cilantro, and lime.

PER SERVING Calories: 243 | Fat: 0.9 g | Protein: 13 g | Sodium: 1,188 mg | Fiber: 7 g | Carbohydrates: 42 g | Sugar: 2.7 g

New Orleans Red Beans and Rice

Red beans and rice is a New Orleans staple that is traditionally served on Mondays.

INGREDIENTS | SERVES 8

¼ cup butter or vegan margarine
1 cup onion, diced
1 cup green bell pepper, diced
1 cup celery, diced
5 cloves garlic, minced
2 (15-ounce) cans red kidney beans, drained
1½ cups water
4 teaspoons salt
2 teaspoons liquid smoke
1 teaspoon vegan Worcestershire sauce
2 teaspoons hot sauce
1 teaspoon dried thyme
2 teaspoons cayenne pepper
4 bay leaves
8 cups cooked long-grain white rice

1. Add the butter or vegan margarine to a 4-quart slow cooker and sauté the onion, green bell pepper, celery, and garlic for 3–5 minutes over high heat.

2. Add the red kidney beans, water, salt, liquid smoke, Worcestershire sauce, hot sauce, dried thyme, cayenne pepper, and bay leaves. Cover and cook on low heat for about 6 hours.

3. Remove the bay leaves and serve over the cooked white rice.

PER SERVING Calories: 397 | Fat: 7 g | Protein: 11 g | Sodium: 1,246 mg | Fiber: 7 g | Carbohydrates: 73 g | Sugar: 3.5 g

Make It "Meaty"

Sausage and ham hocks are the most common meats used in red beans and rice. To make a vegetarian "meaty" version, add cooked, sliced vegetarian sausage and chunks of cooked vegetarian bacon right before serving.

White Beans with Rosemary and Fresh Tomato

Rosemary is a cheap and easy herb to maintain in your garden.

INGREDIENTS | SERVES 8

2 (15-ounce) cans white beans, drained

1 cup water

4 teaspoons salt

3 tablespoons extra-virgin olive oil

4 cloves garlic, minced

2 cups tomatoes, diced

2–3 tablespoons fresh rosemary, chopped

¼ teaspoon black pepper

Add all ingredients to a 4-quart slow cooker. Cover and cook on low heat for about 5–6 hours.

PER SERVING Calories: 163 | Fat: 6 g | Protein: 7 g | Sodium: 1,201.5 mg | Fiber: 6 g | Carbohydrates: 21 g | Sugar: 3 g

Wasabi-Barbecue Chickpeas

Use a store-bought barbecue sauce if you're short on time, but if you do have time to spare, the barbecue sauce recipe in this book will be well worth it.

INGREDIENTS | SERVES 8

1 (16-ounce) bag dried chickpeas
Enough water to cover beans by 1"
2 teaspoons salt
1 onion, diced
2½ tablespoons wasabi powder
3 cups barbecue sauce

Wasabi

Wasabi is a condiment also known as Japanese horseradish or mountain hollyhock, due to the fact that it grows naturally in cool, wet mountain river valleys. It has a spicy and pungent flavor that is known to clear nasal passages if enough is consumed.

1. Rinse the chickpeas, then soak overnight. Drain the water and then rinse the chickpeas again.

2. Add the chickpeas to a large pot and cover with water. Boil on high heat for 10 minutes, then drain.

3. Add chickpeas, water, and salt to a 4-quart slow cooker. Cover and cook on medium heat for about 5–6 hours. Check the beans at about 5 hours and continue cooking if necessary.

4. Once the chickpeas are done, drain in a colander and allow to cool to room temperature.

5. In a large bowl, combine the chickpeas with the rest of the ingredients.

PER SERVING Calories: 232 | Fat: 1 g | Protein: 5 g | Sodium: 1,653 mg | Fiber: 5 g | Carbohydrates: 47 g | Sugar: 25 g

Lentils with Sautéed Spinach, White Wine, and Garlic

Keep a close eye on this one, as spinach takes only a few seconds to sauté perfectly.

INGREDIENTS | SERVES 8

1 (16-ounce) bag dried lentils
Enough water to cover lentils by 1"
4 teaspoons salt
2 tablespoons olive oil
8 cups packed fresh spinach
5 cloves garlic, minced
⅛ cup white wine
1 teaspoon black pepper

1. Add lentils, water, and salt to a 4-quart slow cooker. Cover and cook on medium heat for about 3–4 hours. Check the lentils at about 5 hours and continue cooking if necessary.

2. Once the lentils are done, drain in a colander and allow them to cool to room temperature.

3. While the lentils are cooling, add the olive oil to a large pan and sauté the spinach with the garlic and white wine.

4. In a large bowl, combine the lentils with the sautéed spinach and the remaining salt and pepper.

PER SERVING Calories: 232 | Fat: 4 g | Protein: 15 g | Sodium: 1,207 mg | Fiber: 7 g | Carbohydrates: 35 g | Sugar: 1 g

Chana Masala

The main ingredient in the popular Indian dish chana masala is chickpeas.

INGREDIENTS | SERVES 8

2 (15-ounce) cans chickpeas, drained

1 cup water

4 teaspoons salt

¼ cup butter or vegan margarine

1 onion, diced

5 cloves garlic, minced

1 tablespoon cumin

½ teaspoon cayenne pepper

1 teaspoon ground turmeric

2 teaspoons paprika

1 teaspoon garam masala

1 cup tomatoes, diced

1 lemon, juiced

2 teaspoons grated ginger

Add all ingredients to a 4-quart slow cooker. Cover and cook on low heat for 6 hours.

PER SERVING Calories: 208 | Fat: 7 g | Protein: 7 g | Sodium: 1,210 mg | Fiber: 5 g | Carbohydrates: 30 g | Sugar: 2 g

Indian Cuisine

Due to the size of India and its abundance of spices, Indian cuisine varies by region, community, and religion, but they are all similar. Herbs and spices such as coriander, curry powder, and garam masala are commonly used as well as rice and a variety of lentils.

Easy Edamame

Edamame is baby soybeans, and they're often enjoyed as an appetizer or in salads.

INGREDIENTS | SERVES 8

1 (16-ounce) package frozen edamame, shelled

Enough water to cover edamame by 1"

1 teaspoon coarse sea salt

¼ cup soy sauce

1. Add edamame and water to a 4-quart slow cooker. Cover and cook on high heat for about 1–2 hours. Check the edamame after an hour and continue cooking if necessary.

2. Once the edamame is done, drain in a colander.

3. Sprinkle with coarse sea salt and serve with soy sauce on the side for dipping.

PER SERVING Calories: 158 | Fat: 8 g | Protein: 15 g | Sodium: 748 mg | Fiber: 5 g | Carbohydrates: 14 g | Sugar: 0 g

Summer Vegetable Bean Salad

Serve this salad warm, straight out of the slow cooker, or chilled and over a bed of lettuce.

INGREDIENTS | SERVES 8

1 (15-ounce) can black beans

1 (15-ounce) can red kidney beans

1 (15-ounce) can white beans

1 cup water

4 teaspoons salt

1 red onion, diced

1 green bell pepper, diced

1 red bell pepper, diced

¼ cup cilantro, chopped

½ cup red wine vinegar

½ cup extra-virgin olive oil

1 teaspoon black pepper

Add all ingredients to a 4-quart slow cooker. Cover and cook on low heat for 4 hours.

PER SERVING Calories: 277 | Fat: 14 g | Protein: 9 g | Sodium: 1,359 mg | Fiber: 9 g | Carbohydrates: 26 g | Sugar: 4 g

White Beans

Great northern beans, navy beans, and cannellini beans are all referred to as white beans. Each has its own unique qualities; cannellini beans work best if you want the bean to hold its shape and texture after a long cooking time.

Black Bean Salsa

This recipe makes a lot of salsa, so it's great for parties or large gatherings.

INGREDIENTS | SERVES 8

1 (16-ounce) bag dried black beans
Enough water to cover beans by 1"
4 teaspoons salt
2 (15-ounce) cans tomatoes, drained
1 cup corn
1 onion, diced
1 jalapeño, minced
3 cloves garlic, minced
3 teaspoons apple cider vinegar
2 teaspoons sugar
¼ teaspoon black pepper
¼ cup cilantro, chopped

1. Rinse the black beans, then soak overnight. Drain the water and rinse the beans again.

2. In a large pot, add the beans and cover with water. Boil on high heat for 10 minutes, then drain.

3. Add the black beans, water, and 2 teaspoons salt to a 4-quart slow cooker. Cover and cook on medium heat for about 5–6 hours. Check the beans at about 5 hours and continue cooking if necessary.

4. Once the beans are done, drain in a colander and allow to cool to room temperature.

5. In a large bowl, combine the beans with the rest of the ingredients.

PER SERVING Calories: 109 | Fat: 1 g | Protein: 6 g | Sodium: 1,497 mg | Fiber: 5 g | Carbohydrates: 21 g | Sugar: 5 g

Spicy Black-Eyed Peas and Kale

Black-eyed peas are good sources of fiber, protein, and iron.

INGREDIENTS | SERVES 8

1 (16-ounce) bag dried black-eyed peas

Enough water to cover black-eyed peas by 1"

4 teaspoons salt

2 tablespoons olive oil

1 onion, diced

5 cloves garlic, minced

1 pound kale, chopped

½ teaspoon cayenne pepper

2 teaspoons cumin

1 teaspoon black pepper

1. Rinse the black-eyed peas, then soak overnight. Drain the water and rinse the peas again.

2. In a large pot, add the peas and cover with water. Boil on high heat for 10 minutes, then drain.

3. Add black-eyed peas, water, and 2 teaspoons salt to a 4-quart slow cooker. Cover and cook on medium heat for about 5–6 hours. Check the black-eyed peas at about 5 hours and continue cooking if necessary.

4. Once the black-eyed peas are done, drain in a colander.

5. Add the olive oil to the slow cooker and sauté the onion, garlic, and kale for about 5 minutes.

6. Add the rest of the ingredients, including the black-eyed peas, to the slow cooker. Cover and allow to cook for 15–20 minutes more.

PER SERVING Calories: 257 | Fat: 4.6 g | Protein: 15 g | Sodium: 1,214 mg | Fiber: 7 g | Carbohydrates: 42 g | Sugar: 4.5 g

CHAPTER 11

Tofu

Ginger-Lime Tofu

*The slow cooker does all the work in this recipe, creating a healthy
yet impressive dish that requires virtually no hands-on time.*

INGREDIENTS | SERVES 8

2 (14-ounce) packages extra-firm tofu,
pressed and sliced into fourths
¼ cup minced fresh ginger
¼ cup lime juice
1 lime, thinly sliced
1 onion, thinly sliced

1. Place the tofu filets in a 6- to 7-quart slow cooker. Pour the ginger and lime juice over the tofu, then arrange the lime and then the onion in a single layer over the top.

2. Cook on low for 3–4 hours.

PER SERVING Calories: 75 | Fat: 2 g | Protein: 8 g | Sodium: 63 mg | Fiber: 1 g | Carbohydrates: 6 g | Sugar: 1.8 g

Cracked!

Before each use, check your slow cooker for cracks. Even small cracks in the glaze can allow bacteria to grow in the ceramic insert. If there are cracks, replace the insert or the whole slow cooker.

Tofu Salad Sub

The oil in this recipe can be replaced with mayonnaise or Vegenaise for a creamier texture.

INGREDIENTS | SERVES 4

¼ cup olive oil

1 tablespoon lemon juice

½ teaspoon salt

½ teaspoon pepper

1 clove garlic, minced

¼ cup diced celery

2 teaspoons dried dill

1 (14-ounce) package extra-firm tofu, crumbled

4 hoagie rolls

1. In a small bowl, whisk together the olive oil, lemon juice, salt, pepper, garlic, celery, and dill.

2. Place the crumbled tofu in the bottom of a 2-quart slow cooker, then top with the olive oil and lemon juice blend. Cover and cook on low heat for 2 hours.

3. Place ¼ of the cooked tofu on each of the hoagie rolls, dress with your favorite toppings and serve.

PER SERVING Calories: 261 | Fat: 18 g | Protein: 9.6 g | Sodium: 471.4 mg | Fiber: 2 g | Carbohydrates: 25 g | Sugar: 2.9 g

Tofu Roast

The flavors in this dish resemble those of a classic pot roast.

INGREDIENTS | SERVES 2

1 (14-ounce) package extra-firm tofu, pressed and quartered

4 tablespoons soy sauce

2 tablespoons olive oil

3 potatoes, cubed

3 carrots, peeled and chopped

1 onion, chopped

2 ribs celery, chopped

1 teaspoon salt

¼ teaspoon black pepper

1 tablespoon fresh parsley, chopped

1. Place the tofu and soy sauce in a small bowl and allow to marinate for 10 minutes.

2. Add the rest of the ingredients except for the parsley to a 2-quart slow cooker. Cover and cook on medium heat for 4 hours. Add the parsley to the tofu roast.

PER SERVING Calories: 544 | Fat: 19 g | Protein: 23 g | Sodium: 2,239 mg | Fiber: 10 g | Carbohydrates: 72 g | Sugar: 14 g

Roast Shape

To achieve a more traditionally shaped roast, crumble the tofu, then shape into a loaf using a cheesecloth, pulling tightly to hold the tofu together and remove excess liquid.

Mama's Mock Meatloaf

Crumbled tofu, veggie beef crumbles, or textured vegetable protein will work as the base for this recipe.

INGREDIENTS | SERVES 4

2 (14-ounce) packages extra-firm tofu, pressed and crumbled

¼ cup oats

¼ cup panko bread crumbs

½ cup ketchup

1 teaspoon garlic powder

2 teaspoons vegan Worcestershire sauce

½ onion, diced

3 garlic cloves, minced

½ jalapeño, minced

1 teaspoon salt

½ teaspoon black pepper

1 tablespoon brown sugar

2 teaspoons mustard

1. Add the tofu, oats, bread crumbs, 3 tablespoons ketchup, garlic powder, 1 teaspoon Worcestershire sauce, onion, garlic, jalapeño, salt, and black pepper to a 2-quart slow cooker. Cover and cook on medium heat for 4 hours.

2. In a small bowl, combine the remaining ketchup, Worcestershire sauce, brown sugar, and mustard. Pour the sauce on top of the meatloaf and continue cooking for 20 more minutes.

PER SERVING Calories: 218 | Fat: 6 g | Protein: 16 g | Sodium: 1,075 mg | Fiber: 2 g | Carbohydrates: 25.6 g | Sugar: 13 g

Palak Tofu

Palak tofu is a fresh-tasting, protein-rich Indian dish that is only slightly spicy.

INGREDIENTS | SERVES 4

1 (14-ounce) package extra-firm tofu
1 tablespoon canola oil
1 teaspoon cumin seeds
2 cloves garlic, minced
2 jalapeños, minced
¾ pound red skin potatoes, diced
½ teaspoon ground ginger
¾ teaspoon garam masala
1 pound frozen cut-leaf spinach
¼ cup fresh cilantro

1. Cut the tofu into ½" cubes. Set aside.

2. Heat the oil in a nonstick skillet. Add the cumin seeds and sauté for 1 minute.

3. Add the garlic and jalapeños. Sauté until fragrant, about 1 minute. Add the tofu and potatoes. Sauté for 3 minutes.

4. Add the ginger, garam masala, frozen spinach, and cilantro. Sauté 1 minute.

5. Pour the mixture into a 4-quart slow cooker and cook for 4 hours on low.

PER SERVING Calories: 190 | Fat: 7 g | Protein: 14 g | Sodium: 150 mg | Fiber: 5 g | Carbohydrates: 22 g | Sugar: 3 g

Tofu with Lemon, Capers, and Rosemary

For an even bolder flavor, try marinating the tofu overnight before cooking.

INGREDIENTS | SERVES 4

1 (14-ounce) package extra-firm tofu, pressed and sliced into fourths

⅓ cup water

2 tablespoons lemon juice

1 teaspoon salt

3 thin slices fresh lemon

1 tablespoon nonpareil capers

½ teaspoon minced fresh rosemary

1. Place the tofu filets on the bottom of a 2-quart slow cooker. Pour the water, lemon juice, and salt over the tofu.

2. Arrange the lemon slices in a single layer on top of the tofu. Sprinkle with capers and rosemary.

3. Cover and cook on low for 2 hours. Discard lemon slices prior to serving.

PER SERVING Calories: 63 | Fat: 2.7 g | Protein: 6.9 g | Sodium: 689 mg | Fiber: 0.4 g | Carbohydrates: 3 g | Sugar: 1.4 g

Sweet and Sour Tofu

This recipe is not only kid friendly but vegan and gluten free.
Serve it over rice and garnish with diced green onions.

INGREDIENTS | SERVES 6

12 ounces extra-firm tofu, cubed

¼ cup rice vinegar

3 tablespoons water

1 tablespoon sesame seeds

1 tablespoon brown sugar

1 tablespoon tamari

1 tablespoon pineapple juice

1 teaspoon ground ginger

¾ cup pineapple chunks

1 cup snow peas

½ cup sliced onion

Recipe Variation

For added texture, try breading the tofu with flour or panko bread crumbs and then pan frying it in 2 tablespoons of oil. You can then proceed with the remainder of the recipe.

1. Spray a nonstick skillet with cooking spray. Sauté the tofu until it is lightly browned on each side. Add to a 4-quart slow cooker.

2. In a small bowl, whisk together the vinegar, water, sesame seeds, brown sugar, tamari, pineapple juice, and ginger until the sugar fully dissolves. Pour over the tofu.

3. Add the remaining ingredients.

4. Cover and cook on low for 4 hours. Remove the lid and cook on low for 30 minutes.

PER SERVING   Calories: 101 | Fat: 3 g | Protein: 7 g | Sodium: 210 mg | Fiber: 1 g | Carbohydrates: 10 g | Sugar: 7 g

Thai Tofu Coconut Curry

Try this easy curry tossed with rice noodles or over brown rice.

INGREDIENTS | SERVES 6

12 ounces extra-firm tofu

¼ cup unsweetened shredded coconut

¼ cup water

4 cloves garlic, minced

1 tablespoon minced fresh ginger

1 tablespoon minced galangal root

½ cup chopped onion

1 cup peeled and diced sweet potato

1 cup broccoli florets

1 cup snow peas

3 tablespoons tamari

1 tablespoon vegetarian fish sauce

1 tablespoon chili-garlic sauce

½ cup minced fresh cilantro

½ cup light coconut milk

1. Slice the tofu into ½"-thick triangles.

2. Place the tofu into a 4-quart slow cooker. Top with coconut, water, garlic, ginger, galangal, onion, sweet potato, broccoli, snow peas, tamari, vegetarian fish sauce, and chili-garlic sauce.

3. Stir to distribute all ingredients evenly. Cook on low for 5 hours.

4. Stir in the cilantro and coconut milk. Cook on low for an additional 20 minutes. Stir prior to serving.

PER SERVING Calories: 140 | Fat: 8 g | Protein: 7 g | Sodium: 670 mg | Fiber: 3 g | Carbohydrates: 13 g | Sugar: 3 g

Vegetarian Fish Sauce

Vegetarian fish sauce can be found in some Asian markets or online stores such as VeryAsia.com. Ingredients vary, but it usually contains soy beans, salt, sugar, water, and chili with citric acid for a preservative since it's not fermented.

Tofu Pepper Steak

These "steak" strips make the perfect filling for a sub sandwich.

INGREDIENTS | SERVES 2

1 (14-ounce) package extra-firm tofu, pressed and cut into strips

½ cup soy sauce, divided

3 tablespoons vegetable oil

1 green bell pepper, julienned

1 red bell pepper, julienned

1 onion, julienned

½ teaspoon red pepper flakes

1. In a small bowl, place the tofu and ¼ cup of soy sauce. Allow to marinate for 10 minutes.

2. In a 2-quart slow cooker, place tofu and add all remaining ingredients. Cover and cook on medium heat for 4 hours.

PER SERVING Calories: 376 | Fat: 24 g | Protein: 20 g | Sodium: 1,723 mg | Fiber: 4 g | Carbohydrates: 20 g | Sugar: 9 g

Blackened Tofu

Preparing blackened tofu on the grill is a delicious alternative
to using a slow cooker on a warm summer day.

INGREDIENTS | SERVES 4

2 (14-ounce) packages extra-firm tofu, pressed and quartered

⅓ cup soy sauce

1 tablespoon apple cider vinegar

1 tablespoon garlic, minced

1 tablespoon paprika

2 teaspoons black pepper

1½ teaspoons salt

1 teaspoon garlic powder

1 teaspoon cayenne pepper

½ teaspoon dried oregano

½ teaspoon dried thyme

2 tablespoons vegetable oil

1. Place the tofu, soy sauce, vinegar, and garlic in a small bowl and allow to marinate for 10 minutes.

2. To make the blackened seasoning mixture, combine the paprika, black pepper, salt, garlic powder, cayenne, oregano, and thyme in a small bowl. Remove the tofu from the soy marinade and dip each side into the blackened seasoning.

3. Add the oil and blackened tofu to 2-quart slow cooker. Cover and cook on medium heat for 4 hours.

PER SERVING Calories: 195 | Fat: 10 g | Protein: 16.5 g | Sodium: 1,207 mg | Fiber: 1.5 g | Carbohydrates: 9 g | Sugar: 2.5 g

BBQ Tofu

Crumbled BBQ tofu is best served on a sandwich.
To enjoy it as a main course, skip the crumbling and cook bigger pieces.

INGREDIENTS | SERVES 4

2 (14-ounce) packages extra-firm tofu, pressed and crumbled

1 cup mustard

½ cup sugar

¾ cup apple cider vinegar

¼ cup water

2 tablespoons chili powder

½ teaspoon soy sauce

¼ teaspoon cayenne pepper

2 tablespoons butter or vegan margarine

1 tablespoon liquid smoke

½ teaspoon salt

⅛ teaspoon black pepper

Add all ingredients to a 4-quart slow cooker. Cover and cook on medium heat for 4 hours.

PER SERVING Calories: 333 | Fat: 14 g | Protein: 17 g | Sodium: 1,158 mg | Fiber: 3.5 g | Carbohydrates: 35 g | Sugar: 28 g

Time Saver

To save a little bit of time and money, skip the homemade sauce in this recipe and use bottled barbecue sauce instead. It's easy, cheap, and can still be delicious.

Classic Tofu "Stir-Fry"

Mix and match the vegetables in this all-purpose stir-fry to make your own creation.

INGREDIENTS | SERVES 2

1 red chili pepper, seeded and minced

2 garlic cloves, minced

1 teaspoon ginger, minced

1 tablespoon olive oil

3 tablespoons soy sauce

¼ cup water

1 tablespoon cornstarch

1 (14-ounce) package extra-firm tofu, pressed and cubed

2 tablespoons vegetable oil

2 carrots, cut diagonally

1 red bell pepper, chopped

½ onion, sliced

2 cups bok choy, chopped

½ cup yellow squash, chopped

1. In a medium bowl, combine the chili pepper, garlic, ginger, olive oil, soy sauce, water, and cornstarch. Pour the mixture over the tofu and allow to marinate for 10 minutes.

2. Add the rest of the ingredients to a 4-quart slow cooker. Add the tofu and the rest of the marinade. Cover and cook on medium heat for 4 hours.

PER SERVING Calories: 420 | Fat: 26 g | Protein: 18 g | Sodium: 1,421 mg | Fiber: 5.5 g | Carbohydrates: 29 g | Sugar: 13 g

Cooking with Cornstarch

Cooking with cornstarch can be tricky. To make sure things go smoothly, always combine cornstarch with a liquid before adding it to dry ingredients in a recipe to avoid clumping.

Panang Tofu

Panang is a red curry that is often milder than other curries,
but if you'd like to spice it up, you can add extra peppers.

INGREDIENTS | SERVES 2

1 (14-ounce) package extra-firm tofu, pressed and cubed

1 (13-ounce) can coconut milk

1 tablespoon Panang curry paste

2 tablespoons soy sauce

1 tablespoon lime juice

2 tablespoons sugar

2 tablespoons olive oil

¼ onion, sliced

½ carrot, sliced diagonally

½ red bell pepper, chopped

½ cup fresh basil, chopped

1. Add all ingredients except for the basil to a 4-quart slow cooker.

2. Cover and cook on medium heat for 4 hours.

3. Add the basil before serving.

PER SERVING Calories: 667 | Fat: 56 g | Protein: 20 g | Sodium: 1,169 mg | Fiber: 2 g | Carbohydrates: 28 g | Sugar: 17.5 g

General Tso's Tofu

*The combination of sweet and spicy is what makes this dish a hit
at Chinese restaurants across the country.*

INGREDIENTS | SERVES 2

1 (14-ounce) package of extra-firm tofu, pressed and cubed

1 cup water

2 tablespoons cornstarch

2 cloves garlic, minced

1 teaspoon ginger, minced

⅛ cup sugar

¼ cup soy sauce

⅛ cup white wine vinegar

⅛ cup sherry

2 teaspoons cayenne pepper

2 tablespoons vegetable oil

2 cups broccoli, chopped

Add all ingredients to a 4-quart slow cooker. Cover and cook on medium heat for 4 hours.

PER SERVING Calories: 394 | Fat: 18 g | Protein: 19 g | Sodium: 1,858 mg | Fiber: 3.5 g | Carbohydrates: 36 g | Sugar: 18 g

Kung Pao Tofu

Simplify this dish by using a jar of kung pao sauce from the grocery store.
Most are vegan, but check the label to be sure.

INGREDIENTS | SERVES 2

1 (14-ounce) package extra-firm tofu

2 tablespoons white wine

2 tablespoons soy sauce

2 tablespoons sesame oil

2 tablespoons cornstarch, dissolved in 2 tablespoons water

½ tablespoon hot chili paste

1 teaspoon rice wine vinegar

2 teaspoons brown sugar

½ cup water

1 teaspoon olive oil

½ red bell pepper, chopped

1 clove garlic, minced

¼ cup peanuts

1. In a medium bowl, combine the white wine, soy sauce, sesame oil, cornstarch, chili paste, rice wine vinegar, and brown sugar. Pour the mixture over the tofu and allow to marinate for 10 minutes.

2. Add all ingredients except for the peanuts to a 4-quart slow cooker. Cover and cook on medium heat for 4 hours.

3. Add the peanuts before serving.

PER SERVING Calories: 444 | Fat: 30 g | Protein: 20 g | Sodium: 978 mg | Fiber: 2.5 g | Carbohydrates: 23 g | Sugar: 9 g

CHAPTER 12

Seitan

"Chicken" and Dumplings

Nothing says comfort like creamy dumplings and seitan "chicken."

INGREDIENTS | SERVES 6

2 tablespoons vegetable oil

2 carrots, peeled and diced

2 celery stalks, diced

½ white onion, diced

1 cup frozen peas

1 pound seitan, cubed

6 cups Vegetable Broth (see Chapter 3)

2 teaspoons salt

½ teaspoon pepper

½ teaspoon dried thyme

½ cup unsweetened soymilk

¼ cup flour

1 (10-ounce) package vegan biscuit dough

Make It Vegetarian

For a vegetarian version of this vegan dish, substitute the vegetable broth, soymilk, and flour with 2 cans of cream of mushroom soup.

1. In a sauté pan over medium heat, add the vegetable oil, carrots, celery, and onion, and cook for 3–4 minutes, until soft.

2. Transfer the cooked mixture to a 4-quart slow cooker. Add the frozen peas, seitan, Vegetable Broth, salt, pepper, and thyme.

3. In a small bowl, whisk together the soymilk and flour, then pour into the slow cooker and stir. Cover and cook over low heat for 6 hours.

4. Toward the end of the cooking time, tear each of the biscuits into fourths.

5. Remove the lid and drop in the biscuit dough piece by piece. Cover and cook for an additional 45 seconds.

PER SERVING Calories: 214 | Fat: 12 g | Protein: 16 g | Sodium: 828 mg | Fiber: 3 g | Carbohydrates: 16 g | Sugar: 4 g

Apples-and-Onions Seitan

Try Sonya apples in this sweet and savory dish; they are crisp and sweet.

INGREDIENTS | SERVES 4

4 crisp sweet apples, cut into wedges

2 large onions, sliced

4 equal-sized seitan cutlets (about 1 pound)

½ teaspoon ground cayenne

½ teaspoon ground cinnamon

¼ teaspoon allspice

¼ teaspoon ground fennel

1. Place half of the apple wedges and half of the sliced onions in the bottom of a 4-quart slow cooker. Top with a single layer of seitan.

2. Sprinkle with spices, and top with the remaining apples and onions.

3. Cover and cook on low for 8 hours.

PER SERVING Calories: 178 | Fat: 3.5 g | Protein: 9 g | Sodium: 43 mg | Fiber: 3.5 g | Carbohydrates: 30 g | Sugar: 20 g

Shredded BBQ Seitan

A dash of cayenne pepper and chili powder will add extra heat to this easy dish.

INGREDIENTS | SERVES 8

2 pounds seitan

1 (18-ounce) jar barbecue sauce

Serving Suggestions

Top a toasted sandwich bun with a hefty scoop of barbecue seitan, creamy coleslaw, and a few slices of onions and pickled jalapeños for a kickin' treat.

1. Cut the seitan into thin strips, being sure to vary the size of the pieces and cutting about half so finely that it's shredded.

2. Add the seitan and barbecue sauce to a 4-quart slow cooker. Cover and cook on low heat for 6 hours.

PER SERVING Calories: 193 | Fat: 3 g | Protein: 8 g | Sodium: 745 mg | Fiber: 0.5 g | Carbohydrates: 25 g | Sugar: 18 g

Seitan Fricassee

A fricassee is a versatile dish that is easily adapted for personal taste.
Fennel, mushrooms, or parsnips can be used with great success.

INGREDIENTS | SERVES 6

2 cups sliced red cabbage

2 carrots, cut into coin-sized pieces

2 stalks celery, diced

1 onion, sliced

1 pound seitan, cut into large cubes

¾ cup faux chicken stock

2 teaspoons paprika

2 teaspoons dried thyme

2 teaspoons dried parsley

1. Place the cabbage, carrots, celery, and onions on the bottom of a 4-quart slow cooker. Place the seitan on top of the vegetables.

2. Pour the stock over the seitan and sprinkle it evenly with the spices. Pat the spices onto the seitan.

3. Cook on low 6 hours, or until the seitan is cooked through.

PER SERVING Calories: 107 | Fat: 2.5 g | Protein: 7 g | Sodium: 191 mg | Fiber: 2 g | Carbohydrates: 9.5 g | Sugar: 4 g

Stroganoff

The beef commonly used in stroganoff can be replaced with mushrooms, tempeh, or seitan to create a vegetarian dish.

INGREDIENTS | SERVES 8

1 tablespoon extra-virgin olive oil

1 yellow onion, diced

2 cloves garlic, minced

1 pound seitan, chopped

1 teaspoon salt

4 cups Vegetable Broth (see Chapter 3)

½ cup sour cream or vegan sour cream such as Tofutti Sour Supreme

1 tablespoon ground mustard

¼ cup chopped parsley

1 pound cooked linguine or fettuccine pasta

1. Heat the olive oil in a sauté pan over medium heat. Add the onion and garlic and cook for 2 minutes.

2. Place the sautéed onion and garlic, seitan, salt, and Vegetable Broth in a 4-quart slow cooker. Cover and cook on low for 7 hours.

3. In a small bowl, combine the sour cream, mustard, and parsley, then add to the slow cooker, stirring well.

4. Cover and cook on low for an additional 15 minutes, then serve over cooked pasta.

PER SERVING Calories: 197 g | Fat: 7 g | Protein: 8 g | Sodium: 667 mg | Fiber: 1.5 g | Carbohydrates: 21 g | Sugar: 2 g

Seitan Pot Pie

Morningstar Farms Chik'n Strips are a good alternative to seitan in this recipe.

INGREDIENTS | SERVES 8

1 (16-ounce) package seitan, cut into bite-sized pieces

4 red potatoes, quartered

2 carrots, peeled and chopped

½ cup celery, chopped

½ cup onions, sliced

2 (15-ounce) cans cream of mushroom soup or vegan cream of mushroom soup

2 teaspoons soy sauce

1 teaspoon salt

¼ teaspoon black pepper

Add all the ingredients to a 4-quart slow cooker. Cover and cook on medium heat for 4–5 hours.

PER SERVING Calories: 231 | Fat: 8 g | Protein: 8 g | Sodium: 992 mg | Fiber: 2.5 g | Carbohydrates: 28 g | Sugar: 5 g

Vegan Cream of Mushroom

Make vegan cream of mushroom soup by adding 2 tablespoons of a light roux to 2 cups unsweetened soymilk and then add sautéed mushrooms and onions.

Moroccan "Chicken"

This dish was inspired by traditional North African tagines and adapted for the slow cooker.

INGREDIENTS | SERVES 8

½ teaspoon coriander

½ teaspoon cinnamon

¼ teaspoon salt

1 teaspoon cumin

2 pounds seitan, cubed

½ cup water

4 cloves garlic, minced

1 onion, thinly sliced

1 knob ginger, minced

1 (15-ounce) can chickpeas, drained and rinsed

4 ounces dried apricots, halved

1. Place all of the spices, seitan, water, garlic, onion, and ginger into a 4-quart slow cooker. Cook on low for 5 hours.

2. Stir in the chickpeas and apricots and cook on high for 40 minutes.

PER SERVING Calories: 323 | Fat: 6 g | Protein: 19 g | Sodium: 129 mg | Fiber: 11 g | Carbohydrates: 45 g | Sugar: 15 g

Moroccan Cuisine

Moroccan cuisine uses many different spices. Some of the most common are cumin, cinnamon, turmeric, saffron, and paprika. Traditional Moroccan food is served in a communal bowl at a low, round table. Diners take food from the bowl using pieces of bread or their hands.

Red Wine "Pot Roast"

A little bit of wine goes a long way in flavoring this simple one-crock meal.

INGREDIENTS | SERVES 6

⅓ cup red wine
½ cup water
4 red skin potatoes, quartered
3 carrots, cut into thirds
2 bulbs fennel, quartered
2 rutabagas, quartered
1 onion, sliced
4 cloves garlic, sliced
1½ pounds seitan, cubed
½ teaspoon salt
½ teaspoon freshly ground black pepper

1. Pour the wine and water into a 4-quart slow cooker. Add the potatoes, carrots, fennel, rutabagas, onion, and garlic. Stir.

2. Add the seitan. Sprinkle with salt and pepper. Cover and cook on low for 8 hours.

PER SERVING Calories: 378 | Fat: 12 g | Protein: 20 g | Sodium: 300 mg | Fiber: 11 g | Carbohydrates: 49 g | Sugar: 11 g

Spiced Apple Cider Seitan

This recipe makes candied sweet potatoes while it cooks the seitan in the sweetened cider sauce.

INGREDIENTS | SERVES 8

3 pounds seitan, cubed

Salt and freshly ground black pepper, to taste

2 apples, peeled, cored, and sliced

4 large sweet potatoes, peeled and cut in half

½ cup apple cider or apple juice

½ teaspoon ground cinnamon

¼ teaspoon ground cloves

¼ teaspoon ground allspice

2 tablespoons brown sugar

1. Treat the crock of a 4-quart slow cooker with nonstick spray.

2. Add seitan and season it with salt and pepper.

3. Arrange apple slices over and around the seitan. Add the sweet potatoes.

4. In a bowl or measuring cup, stir together the cider or juice, cinnamon, cloves, allspice, and brown sugar. Pour over the ingredients in the slow cooker.

5. Cover and cook on low for 8 hours.

PER SERVING Calories: 369 | Fat: 17 g | Protein: 23 g | Sodium: 60 mg | Fiber: 4.5 g | Carbohydrates: 37 g | Sugar: 13 g

Vegan Ropa Vieja

Serve this Cuban dish with yellow rice and Cuban Black Beans.

INGREDIENTS | SERVES 8

2 pounds seitan, cubed

1 cubanelle pepper, diced

1 large onion, diced

2 carrots, diced

28 ounces canned crushed tomatoes

2 cloves garlic

1 tablespoon oregano

½ teaspoon cumin

½ cup sliced green olives stuffed with pimento

1. Place the seitan, pepper, onions, carrots, tomatoes, garlic, oregano, and cumin into a 2-quart slow cooker. Cook on high for 7 hours.

2. Add the olives and continue to cook for 20 minutes.

3. Shred the seitan with a fork, knife, or grater, then mash it with a potato masher until very well mixed.

PER SERVING Calories: 210 | Fat: 12 g | Protein: 15.5 g | Sodium: 229 mg | Fiber: 3 g | Carbohydrates: 14 g | Sugar: 4 g

Seitan with White Wine and Garlic

Seitan in a white wine sauce goes perfectly with a side of crisp asparagus and rice.

INGREDIENTS | SERVES 8

2 tablespoons olive oil

6 cloves garlic, smashed

½ onion, diced

2 pounds seitan

1 cup white wine

1 cup Vegetable Broth (see Chapter 3)

1 lemon, halved and juiced

1 bay leaf

2 sprigs fresh thyme

Salt and pepper, to taste

1. Add the olive oil to a 4-quart slow cooker and bring to medium heat. Add the garlic and onion and cook for 5 minutes, stirring occasionally.

2. Add the seitan, white wine, Vegetable Broth, lemon halves and lemon juice, bay leaf, and thyme. Cover and cook over low heat for 6 hours. Season with salt and pepper, to taste, before serving.

PER SERVING Calories: 292 | Fat: 16.5 g | Protein: 17 g | Sodium: 171 mg | Fiber: 1 g | Carbohydrates: 17 g | Sugar: 3 g

Seitan Sandwich Meat

Use a block or ball of seitan for this recipe, not cubes or shredded pieces.

INGREDIENTS | SERVES 8

4 cups Vegetable Broth (see Chapter 3)
1 teaspoon salt
2 teaspoons pepper
2 teaspoons garlic powder
2 teaspoons onion powder
1 teaspoon dried oregano
1 teaspoon soy sauce
1 teaspoon liquid smoke
2 pounds seitan, divided into 2 large pieces

1. Combine all ingredients except for the seitan in a 4-quart slow cooker, stirring well.

2. Add the seitan. Cover and cook on medium heat for 6 hours.

3. Remove the seitan from the liquid and once cool, slice into thin sandwich slices.

PER SERVING Calories: 171 | Fat: 11 g | Protein: 14.5 g | Sodium: 338 mg | Fiber: 1 g | Carbohydrates: 6.5 g | Sugar: 0 g

Mix It Up

Spice this recipe up by adding an additional teaspoon of cayenne or chipotle pepper. Another recipe variation is to make it more Italian by omitting soy sauce and adding a handful of fresh basil instead.

Salsa Seitan

These easy seitan strips make the perfect filling for tacos and burritos or can be used in vegetarian fajitas.

INGREDIENTS | SERVES 8

2 pounds seitan, cut into ½" strips
2 cups salsa

Choosing Salsa

Salsa recipes vary greatly in taste and texture, so be sure to choose the right salsa for your dish. If you'll be topping the seitan strips with fresh ingredients such as red onion, cilantro, and lime juice, tomatillo salsa is a complementary salsa.

1. Coat a 4-quart slow cooker with nonstick spray.

2. Add the seitan strips, then top with salsa.

3. Cover and cook on low heat for 6 hours.

PER SERVING Calories: 181 | Fat: 11 g | Protein: 15 g | Sodium: 390 mg | Fiber: 1.7 g | Carbohydrates: 9 g | Sugar: 2 g

Broccoli, Snow Peas, and Seitan

Stir-fry-like dishes can be made in a slow cooker. Just add a side of rice or noodles, and serve.

INGREDIENTS | SERVES 8

2 pounds seitan, cut into ½" strips

½ cup soy sauce

½ cup water

1 tablespoon sesame oil

1 teaspoon sugar

2 cloves garlic, minced

1 teaspoon cornstarch

1 teaspoon warm water

1 cup broccoli florets

1 cup snow peas

1. Placed the seitan strips in a 4-quart slow cooker. In a small bowl, whisk together the soy sauce, water, sesame oil, sugar, and garlic, then pour over the seitan. Cover and cook on low heat for 6 hours.

2. In a small bowl, whisk together the cornstarch and 1 teaspoon warm water, then add to the slow cooker, stirring until well combined.

3. Add the broccoli and snow peas. Cover and cook for an additional 15 minutes.

PER SERVING Calories: 208 | Fat: 13 g | Protein: 15.5 g | Sodium: 905 mg | Fiber: 1.5 g | Carbohydrates: 8.5 g | Sugar: 1.5 g

Cheesy Seitan Pasta

During the last 45 minutes of cooking, throw in broccoli florets or peas to increase the nutritional value of this dish.

INGREDIENTS | SERVES 4–6

1 teaspoon warm water

1 teaspoon cornstarch

3 cups 2% milk or unsweetened soymilk

2 cups Cheddar cheese or vegan Cheddar such as Daiya Cheddar Style Shreds

1 pound seitan, shredded

½ pound macaroni pasta

1. In a small bowl, whisk together the warm water and cornstarch.

2. Pour the cornstarch mixture into a 4-quart slow cooker, then add the soymilk, cheese, seitan, and macaroni.

3. Cover and cook on low heat for 6 hours.

PER SERVING Calories: 475 | Fat: 24 g | Protein: 27 g | Sodium: 290 mg | Fiber: 1.5 g | Carbohydrates: 37 g | Sugar: 7.5 g

Making Your Own Seitan

Seitan, also called wheat gluten or wheat-meat, can be made at home by rinsing wheat flour thoroughly until all of the starch dissolves, leaving you with raw gluten that is ready to be simmered in broth or baked. For complete directions, see *www.ehow.com/how_5157979_make-vital-wheat-gluten.html*

Jerk Seitan

Many jerk recipes call for rubbing the spice mixture into the protein before cooking, but in a slow cooker that step isn't necessary.

INGREDIENTS | SERVES 4

1 pound shredded seitan

½ cup Vegetable Broth (see Chapter 3)

½ teaspoon allspice

¼ teaspoon cinnamon

½ teaspoon dried thyme

¼ teaspoon ground nutmeg

1 teaspoon salt

¼ cup red onion, diced

2 cloves garlic, minced

2 tablespoons fresh jalapeño, seeded and minced

1. Prepare a 4-quart slow cooker with nonstick cooking spray, then add the shredded seitan.

2. In a medium bowl, combine all remaining ingredients, then pour over the seitan.

3. Cover and cook on low for 6 hours.

PER SERVING Calories: 174 | Fat: 11 g | Protein: 14.5 g | Sodium: 556 mg | Fiber: 1 g | Carbohydrates: 7 g | Sugar: 0.5 g

Seitan Marinara

This is a great sauce for a Sunday meal that the entire family will enjoy.

INGREDIENTS | SERVES 8

2 tablespoons olive oil

½ onion, diced

2 cloves garlic, minced

1 (16-ounce) package seitan, cut into small pieces

2 (14-ounce) cans diced tomatoes

½ teaspoon sugar

1 tablespoon tomato paste

⅓ cup water

1 lemon, juiced

2 tablespoons fresh basil, chopped

1 teaspoon salt

¼ teaspoon black pepper

1. Add the olive oil to a 4-quart slow cooker and sauté the onion and garlic on medium heat for about 3 minutes.

2. Add the rest of the ingredients. Cover and cook on medium heat for 2 hours.

PER SERVING Calories: 148 | Fat: 9 g | Protein: 8 g | Sodium: 317 mg | Fiber: 2 g | Carbohydrates: 9 g | Sugar: 3.5 g

Seitan Po Boys

Po Boys are submarine sandwiches from Louisiana that usually contain roasted meat or fried seafood.

INGREDIENTS | SERVES 8

3 tablespoons olive oil

1 (16-ounce) package seitan, cut into bite-sized pieces

½ cup water

⅛ cup Old Bay seasoning

1 teaspoon salt

¼ teaspoon black pepper

4–6 French bread rolls

2 cups lettuce, shredded

1 tomato, sliced

16 dill pickle slices

¼ cup mayonnaise or vegan mayonnaise

1. Add olive oil, seitan, water, Old Bay seasoning, salt, and pepper to a 4-quart slow cooker. Cover and cook on medium heat for 1 hour.

2. Serve seitan on French bread rolls with lettuce, tomato, pickle, and mayonnaise.

PER SERVING Calories: 283 | Fat: 17.5 g | Protein: 9.5 g | Sodium: 667 mg | Fiber: 1.5 g | Carbohydrates: 24 g | Sugar: 10.5 g

New Orleans Fast Food

The Po Boy continues to be the most popular sandwich in New Orleans. Many locals consume at least one per week because of its convenience, price, and, well, because it's just good.

Spicy Seitan Tacos

Hard or soft taco shells work well with this tasty recipe.

INGREDIENTS | SERVES 8

2 tablespoons olive oil

1 (16-ounce) package seitan, chopped into small pieces

2 cloves garlic, minced

½ cup soy sauce

1 tablespoon chili powder

¼ teaspoon chipotle powder

¼ teaspoon garlic powder

¼ teaspoon crushed red pepper flakes

¼ teaspoon onion powder

2 teaspoons cumin

½ teaspoon paprika

1 teaspoon salt

1 teaspoon black pepper

8 taco shells

1 cup shredded Cheddar or vegan Cheddar cheese

1 cup lettuce, shredded

1 tomato, diced

1. Add all the ingredients, except for shells, cheese, lettuce, and tomatoes, to a 4-quart slow cooker. Cover and cook on medium heat for 1 hour.

2. Serve the seitan in the shells and top with cheese, lettuce, and tomato.

PER SERVING Calories: 250 | Fat: 16.5 g | Protein: 13 g | Sodium: 1,246 mg | Fiber: 2 g | Carbohydrates: 14 g | Sugar: 1 g

Fresh Tortillas

For an extra special treat, try fresh tortillas. You may have to do a little hunting around, but they can often be found at international farmer's markets and Latino stores.

French Dip Seitan Sandwiches

*Melt some provolone or vegan cheese on your sandwiches
to make these French dips even more delicious.*

INGREDIENTS | SERVES 8

1 (16-ounce) package seitan, thinly sliced
2 quarts vegetarian "beef" broth
8–12 pieces sliced bread

Ways to Serve French Dip

The original French dip was served on a roll
that was dipped in au jus and served wet.
Most restaurants now serve the sandwich
on a baguette with the au jus on the side.

1. Add the seitan and broth to a 4-quart slow cooker.
   Cover and cook on medium heat for 2 hours.

2. Place the seitan on the bread and assemble the French
   dip sandwiches. Serve the extra broth in ramekins for
   dipping.

PER SERVING Calories: 191 | Fat: 6.5 g | Protein: 13.5 g |
Sodium: 991 mg | Fiber: 1 g | Carbohydrates: 20.5 g | Sugar: 1 g

CHAPTER 13

Tempeh

Ginger-Soy Tempeh Cubes

*Tempeh is made from fermented soybeans, and is used
as a meat replacement in many vegetarian dishes.*

INGREDIENTS | SERVES 4

3 cloves garlic, minced

1 tablespoon fresh ginger, minced

1 cup soy sauce

1 cup water

2 limes, juiced

¼ cup olive oil

2 tablespoons sugar

1 (13-ounce) package tempeh, cut into bite-sized squares

3 green onions, sliced

1. In a small bowl, combine garlic, ginger, soy sauce, water, lime juice, olive oil, and sugar.

2. Add all ingredients, except for the green onions, to a 4-quart slow cooker. Cover and cook on medium heat for 4 hours. Garnish with the green onions.

PER SERVING Calories: 370 | Fat: 23 g | Protein: 21 g | Sodium: 2,305 mg | Fiber: 1.5 g | Carbohydrates: 24 g | Sugar: 8.5 g

Tempeh and Gravy

Tempeh and gravy is delicious for breakfast, lunch, or dinner!

INGREDIENTS | SERVES 4

½ cup vegetable oil

3 cloves garlic, minced

¼ cup onion, minced

½ cup flour

⅛ cup nutritional yeast

¼ cup soy sauce

2 cups water

½ teaspoon sage

¼ teaspoon black pepper

1 (13-ounce) package tempeh, cut into bite-sized squares

1. Add all ingredients, except for the tempeh, to a 4-quart slow cooker. Cook on medium heat for about 10 minutes, stirring continuously.

2. Add the tempeh, cover, and cook on medium heat for 2–3 hours.

PER SERVING Calories: 504 | Fat: 37 g | Protein: 22 g | Sodium: 1,235 mg | Fiber: 1 g | Carbohydrates: 24 g | Sugar: 0.5 g

Nutritional Yeast

Nutritional yeast, an inactive yeast, is a staple in many vegan kitchens. Because it is inactive, it won't make things rise and should not be used for baking. It is often used to make cheese-style sauces due to its nutty, cheesey flavor. As a bonus, some brands are fortified with vitamin B_{12}.

Curried Tempeh in Coconut Cream

Try serving Curried Tempeh over rice or in cool, crisp lettuce leaves.

INGREDIENTS | SERVES 4

2 cloves garlic, minced

1 teaspoon fresh ginger, minced

¾ cup soy sauce

1 tablespoon vegetable oil

1 tablespoon Sriracha sauce

1 (13-ounce) can coconut milk

1 cup water

1 (13-ounce) package tempeh, cut into bite-sized sqaures

¼ cup fresh basil, chopped

1. Add all ingredients, except for the basil, to a 4-quart slow cooker. Cover, and cook on medium heat for 4 hours.

2. About 10 minutes before the tempeh is done cooking, stir in the basil, cook for the remaining time, and serve.

PER SERVING Calories: 412 | Fat: 32 g | Protein: 22 g | Sodium: 2315 mg | Fiber: 0.5 g | Carbohydrates: 15 g | Sugar: 0.5 g

Orange Wasabi Soy Tempeh

Agave nectar, a honey alternative for vegans, and tequila are made from the same plant, but couldn't be more different.

INGREDIENTS | SERVES 4

2 cups orange juice

1 cup agave nectar

½ cup soy sauce

Juice of 2 limes

½ teaspoon wasabi powder

1 cup water

1 (13-ounce) package tempeh, cut into bite-sized squares

1. In a medium bowl, combine all ingredients except for the tempeh.

2. Add all ingredients to a 4-quart slow cooker. Cover and cook on medium heat for 4 hours.

PER SERVING Calories: 511 | Fat: 10 g | Protein: 20 g | Sodium: 1,350 mg | Fiber: 1 g | Carbohydrates: 95 g | Sugar: 80 g

Hoisin-Glazed Tempeh

Hoisin is a strongly flavored, slightly spicy and slightly sweet Chinese sauce.

INGREDIENTS | SERVES 4

1 (13-ounce) package tempeh, cut into bite-sized squares

4 cloves garlic, minced

2 teaspoons fresh ginger, minced

1½ cups soy sauce

1 cup hoisin sauce

1 cup water

3 tablespoons fresh lime juice

Serving Suggestions

For a traditional dish, serve this tempeh over steamed rice or noodles. If you want to be a little more adventurous, use it as a taco filling or as a filling for a folded flat bread.

Add all ingredients to a 4-quart slow cooker. Cover and cook on medium heat for 4 hours.

PER SERVING Calories: 372 | Fat: 12 g | Protein: 25 g | Sodium: 5,402 mg | Fiber: 2.5 g | Carbohydrates: 45 g | Sugar: 19 g

Lemon-Pepper Tempeh

When fresh herbs are in season, add chopped curly or flat-leaf parsley to this dish before serving.

INGREDIENTS | SERVES 4

1 (13-ounce) package tempeh, cut into bite-sized squares

6 cloves garlic, minced

1 teaspoon fresh ginger, minced

½ cup water

1 cup soy sauce

½ cup extra-virgin olive oil

¼ cup fresh lemon juice

1 teaspoon black pepper

Add all ingredients to a 4-quart slow cooker. Cover and cook on medium heat for 4 hours.

PER SERVING Calories: 455 | Fat: 36 g | Protein: 21 g | Sodium: 3,608 mg | Fiber: 0.5 g | Carbohydrates: 15 g | Sugar: 1 g

Serving Suggestions

Make this tempeh dish the star of the show and serve as a main course, with a vegetable and grain on the side. Or, place the strips on a hoagie roll topped with mayonnaise or vegan mayonnaise and lettuce to make a tasty sub sandwich.

Carolina-Style Barbecue Tempeh

Vinegar-based barbecue sauce, as opposed to tomato-based, is popular across the South.

INGREDIENTS | SERVES 4

4 cloves garlic, minced

2 teaspoons fresh ginger, minced

1 cup soy sauce

½ cup apple cider vinegar

½ cup maple syrup

½ cup olive oil

2 teaspoons chipotle powder

1 teaspoon dried thyme

1 teaspoon paprika

1 teaspoon cumin

¼ teaspoon black pepper

1 (13-ounce) package tempeh, cut into bite-sized squares

4 hamburger buns

1. In a small bowl, combine all ingredients except for the tempeh and hamburger buns.

2. Add all ingredients, except for the hamburger buns, to a 4-quart slow cooker. Cover, and cook on medium heat for 4 hours. Serve on the hamburger buns.

PER SERVING Calories: 650 | Fat: 38 g | Protein: 23 g | Sodium: 3,718 mg | Fiber: 2.5 g | Carbohydrates: 57 g | Sugar: 26 g

Tempeh Bacon

Save money by making your own tempeh bacon instead of buying it prepackaged in stores.

INGREDIENTS | SERVES 4

2 cloves garlic, minced

1 teaspoon fresh ginger, minced

¾ cup soy sauce

½ cup water

1 tablespoon maple syrup

½ teaspoon garlic powder

1 tablespoon liquid smoke

2 tablespoons vegetable oil

1 (13-ounce) package tempeh, cut into bite-sized squares

1. In a small bowl, add all ingredients except for the tempeh. Stir well to combine.

2. Add all ingredients to a 4-quart slow cooker. Cover and cook on medium heat for 4 hours.

PER SERVING Calories: 275 | Fat: 16.5 g | Protein: 20 g | Sodium: 2,204 mg | Fiber: 0.5 g | Carbohydrates: 16 g | Sugar: 4 g

Liquid Smoke

Liquid smoke is a concentrated sauce made from the smoke of burning wood chips. It is a great way to add depth to vegetables, such as collard greens.

General Tso's Tempeh

General Tso's chicken is the inspiration for this vegetarian version.
Surprisingly, the Chinese dish is rumored to have originated in the United States.

INGREDIENTS | SERVES 4

4 cloves garlic, minced

3 teaspoons fresh ginger, minced

¾ cup soy sauce

2 tablespoons cornstarch

1 cup boiling water

¼ cup sugar

⅛ cup white wine vinegar

⅛ cup sherry

2 teaspoons red pepper flakes

2 cups broccoli, chopped

2 carrots, sliced

1 (13-ounce) package tempeh, cut into bite-sized pieces

1. In a medium bowl, combine the garlic, ginger, soy sauce, cornstarch, water, sugar, vinegar, sherry, and red pepper flakes.

2. Add all ingredients to a 4-quart slow cooker. Cover and cook on medium heat for 4 hours.

PER SERVING Calories: 311 | Fat: 10 g | Protein: 21 g | Sodium: 2,454 mg | Fiber: 3 g | Carbohydrates: 36 g | Sugar: 16.5 g

Spicy Tempeh Tacos

Hard taco shells or soft taco shells both work for this recipe. The only difference is that each requires different cooking times and methods, so be sure to read the package directions.

INGREDIENTS | SERVES 4

1 (13-ounce) package tempeh

2 cloves garlic, minced

1 teaspoon fresh ginger, minced

½ cup soy sauce

1 cup water

1 tablespoon chili powder

¼ teaspoon chipotle powder

¼ teaspoon garlic powder

¼ teaspoon crushed red pepper flakes

¼ teaspoon onion powder

2 teaspoons cumin

½ teaspoon paprika

1 teaspoon salt

¼ teaspoon black pepper

8 taco shells

1 cup shredded Cheddar cheese or vegan Cheddar

1 cup lettuce, shredded

1 tomato, diced

1. Add the tempeh, garlic, ginger, soy sauce, water, chili powder, chipotle powder, garlic powder, red pepper flakes, cumin, paprika, salt, and black pepper to a 4-quart slow cooker. Cover and cook on medium heat for 4 hours.

2. Serve the tempeh in taco shells and garnish with cheese, lettuce, and tomato.

PER SERVING Calories: 440 | Fat: 24 g | Protein: 28 g | Sodium: 2,477 mg | Fiber: 2 g | Carbohydrates: 30 g | Sugar: 2 g

Simplify This Recipe

The only required spices for the tempeh are some type of pepper, cumin, and salt, so even if you don't have all of the ingredients listed, you can still create a delicious dish.

Spicy Tempeh Fajitas

Add a dollop of sour cream or soy sour cream and salsa to finish off each of your fajitas.

INGREDIENTS | SERVES 4

1 (13-ounce) package tempeh, cut into bite-sized pieces

2 cloves garlic, minced

1 teaspoon fresh ginger, minced

½ cup soy sauce

1 cup water

1 tablespoon olive oil

½ teaspoon chili powder

¼ teaspoon chipotle powder

1 teaspoon salt

¼ teaspoon black pepper

½ onion, sliced

½ green bell pepper, sliced

1 jalapeño, minced

½ cup mushrooms, sliced

8–12 corn tortillas

1 tomato, diced

¼ cup cilantro, chopped

1 lime, cut into wedges

1. Add the tempeh, garlic, ginger, soy sauce, water, olive oil, chili powder, chipotle powder, salt, and black pepper, onion, green bell pepper, jalapeño, and mushrooms to a 4-quart slow cooker. Cover and cook on medium heat for 4 hours.

2. Serve the fajitas on the tortillas and garnish with tomato, cilantro, and lime.

PER SERVING Calories: 361 | Fat: 15 g | Protein: 23 g | Sodium: 2,323 mg | Fiber: 5 g | Carbohydrates: 39 g | Sugar: 3 g

Tempeh Sliders

Sliders are mini sandwiches, perfect as an appetizer or a snack.

INGREDIENTS | SERVES 4

1 (13-ounce) package tempeh, cut into 8 squares

2 cloves garlic, minced

1 teaspoon fresh ginger, minced

½ cup soy sauce

1 cup water

1 teaspoon salt

¼ teaspoon black pepper

½ teaspoon garlic powder

½ teaspoon onion powder

¼ teaspoon cumin

⅛ teaspoon cayenne pepper

2 teaspoons olive oil

½ onion, sliced

6–8 slices American cheese or vegan Cheddar

8 mini sandwich buns

1. Add the tempeh, garlic, ginger, soy sauce, water, salt, black pepper, garlic powder, onion powder, cumin, and cayenne pepper to a 4-quart slow cooker. Cover and cook on medium heat for 4 hours.

2. About 5 minutes before the sliders are done cooking, add the olive oil to a pan and sauté the onions over medium-high heat until they are soft, about 5 minutes.

3. Melt a slice of cheese on each piece of tempeh and top with the onions. Serve on mini sandwich buns.

PER SERVING Calories: 583 | Fat: 26 g | Protein: 34 g | Sodium: 2,980 mg | Fiber: 6.5 g | Carbohydrates: 59 g | Sugar: 8 g

Finding Vegan Bread

Some bread recipes call for eggs, dairy, and honey, but there are also many that do not, and finding vegan sandwich buns shouldn't be a challenge. Some grocery stores such as Kroger even label Kroger-brand bread as vegan, if it is.

Tempeh, Fresh Tomato, and Basil Scramble

Red wine vinegar and basil give this tempeh scramble a Mediterranean flavor.

INGREDIENTS | SERVES 4

1 (13-ounce) package tempeh, cubed

1½ cups olive oil

½ cup red wine vinegar

½ cup water

4 cloves garlic, minced

½ red onion, diced

1 teaspoon salt

¼ teaspoon red pepper

2 fresh tomatoes, diced

¼ cup basil, chopped

1. Add the tempeh, olive oil, red wine vinegar, water, garlic, red onion, salt, and pepper to a 4-quart slow cooker. Cover and cook on medium heat for 4 hours.

2. When the tempeh is done cooking, allow to cool to room temperature. Then, toss with the tomatoes and basil.

PER SERVING Calories: 918 | Fat: 90 g | Protein: 17 g | Sodium: 605 mg | Fiber: 1 g | Carbohydrates: 13 g | Sugar: 2 g

Tempeh "Stir-Fry"

Soy sauce is the classic base for a stir-fry dish.

INGREDIENTS | SERVES 4

1 (13-ounce) package tempeh, cut into bite-sized squares

6 cloves garlic

2 cups vegetarian "chicken" broth

¼ cup soy sauce

1 tablespoon brown sugar

¼ teaspoon Sriracha sauce

1 lime, juiced

2 carrots, sliced

½ onion, sliced

2 cups broccoli, chopped

4 cups cooked brown rice

1. Add all ingredients, except for the rice, to a 4-quart slow cooker. Cover and cook on medium heat for 4 hours.

2. Serve each serving of tempeh over 1 cup of rice.

PER SERVING Calories: 457 | Fat: 12 g | Protein: 24 g | Sodium: 950 mg | Fiber: 6 g | Carbohydrates: 68 g | Sugar: 6.5 g

White Rice Versus Brown Rice

There are many varieties of both white rice and brown rice. but one of the common differences is that brown rice is more nutritious, containing magnesium, B vitamins, and iron.

"Short Rib" Tempeh

No pigs necessary for this mouthwatering "rib" recipe!

INGREDIENTS | SERVES 4

1 (13-ounce) package tempeh, cut into strips

1 (28-ounce) can tomato sauce

½ cup water

⅛ cup vegan Worcestershire sauce

2 tablespoons brown sugar

2 tablespoons dried parsley

1 teaspoon Tabasco sauce

1 teaspoon salt

¼ teaspoon black pepper

1 lemon, juiced

1 tablespoon soy sauce

Add all ingredients to a 4-quart slow cooker. Cover and cook on low heat for 6 hours.

PER SERVING Calories: 264 | Fat: 10 g | Protein: 20 g | Sodium: 1,946 mg | Fiber: 3.5 g | Carbohydrates: 29 g | Sugar: 16 g

"Buffalo"-Style Tempeh

This recipe makes appetizer-size servings, not full entrée-size servings.

INGREDIENTS | SERVES 8

1 (13-ounce) package tempeh, cut into strips

1 cup butter or vegan margarine, melted

1 cup Tabasco sauce

3 stalks of celery, cut into strips

1 cup blue cheese dressing or vegan ranch dressing

Vegan Ranch

Vegan ranch dressing is sold in some grocery stores and can be ordered online. Try OrganVille's Dairy-Free Ranch as a delicious alternative to traditional ranch.

1. Add the tempeh, butter or margarine, and Tabasco sauce to a 4-quart slow cooker. Cover and cook on medium heat for 4 hours.

2. Serve on a platter with the celery sticks and dressing.

PER SERVING Calories: 439 | Fat: 43 g | Protein: 10 g | Sodium: 476 mg | Fiber: 0.5 g | Carbohydrates: 6.5 g | Sugar: 1.5 g

Indian Curry Tempeh

Any type of curry powder you have on hand will work in this recipe, but madras curry powder is best.

INGREDIENTS | SERVES 4

1 (13-ounce) package tempeh, cut into bite-sized squares

3 cloves garlic, minced

1 teaspoon ginger, minced

1 onion, sliced

2 carrots, peeled and julienned

1 cup cauliflower, chopped

⅓ cup tomato paste

1 (15-ounce) can coconut milk

1 cup water

¼ cup curry powder

1 (15-ounce) can chickpeas, drained

1 teaspoon salt

¼ teaspoon black pepper

Add all ingredients to a 4-quart slow cooker. Cover and cook on medium heat for 4 hours.

PER SERVING Calories: 636 | Fat: 36 g | Protein: 31 g | Sodium: 834 mg | Fiber: 13.5 g | Carbohydrates: 57 g | Sugar: 11 g

Tempeh Reuben Sandwiches

Some grocery store-brand Thousand Island Dressings are "accidentally vegan," just be sure to read the label.

INGREDIENTS | SERVES 6

1 (13-ounce) package tempeh, cut into strips

1 cup water

¼ cup apple cider vinegar

2 tablespoons paprika

1 tablespoon dried oregano

¼ cup Dijon mustard

¼ teaspoon liquid smoke

2 teaspoons allspice

3 cloves garlic, minced

1 teaspoon salt

¼ teaspoon black pepper

12 slices rye bread

1 cup sauerkraut

6 slices Swiss cheese or vegan Cheddar

½ cup Thousand Island dressing

1. Add the tempeh, water, apple cider vinegar, paprika, oregano, Dijon mustard, liquid smoke, allspice, garlic, salt, and pepper to a 4-quart slow cooker. Cover and cook on medium heat for 4 hours.

2. Serve on the rye bread with sauerkraut, cheese, and Thousand Island dressing.

PER SERVING Calories: 500 | Fat: 26 g | Protein: 25 g | Sodium: 1,327 mg | Fiber: 5 g | Carbohydrates: 43 g | Sugar: 6.5 g

Tempeh and Baby Bok Choy Scramble

Bok choy is also called Chinese cabbage, and if you can't find bok choy, cabbage will do.

INGREDIENTS | SERVES 4

1 (13-ounce) package tempeh, cut into bite-sized squares

2–3 heads baby bok choy, leaves cut into bite-sized pieces

1 onion, sliced

1 red pepper, chopped

3 cloves garlic, minced

1 cup vegetarian "chicken" broth

¼ teaspoon red pepper flakes

1 teaspoon salt

¼ teaspoon black pepper

Add all ingredients to a 4-quart slow cooker. Cover and cook on low heat for 6 hours.

PER SERVING Calories: 276 | Fat: 11 g | Protein: 26 g | Sodium: 1,009 mg | Fiber: 7 g | Carbohydrates: 26 g | Sugar: 8 g

Sweet and Sour Tempeh

Ketchup is a surprise ingredient in this sweet and sour sauce.

INGREDIENTS | SERVES 4

½ cup white sugar

2 tablespoons pineapple juice

⅓ cup white vinegar

1 cup water

2 tablespoons soy sauce

2 tablespoons vegan Worcestershire sauce

¼ cup ketchup

2 tablespoons cornstarch

1 (13-ounce) package tempeh, cut into bite-sized squares

1. In a medium bowl, combine the white sugar, pineapple juice, white vinegar, water, soy sauce, Worcestershire sauce, ketchup, and cornstarch.

2. Add all ingredients to a 4-quart slow cooker. Cover and cook on medium heat for 4 hours.

PER SERVING Calories: 321 | Fat: 9.5 g | Protein: 17.5 g | Sodium: 709 mg | Fiber: 0 g | Carbohydrates: 44 g | Sugar: 30 g

Cottage Pie with Carrots, Parsnips, and Celery

Cottage Pie is similar to the more familiar Shepherd's Pie, but this version uses tempeh instead of meat.

INGREDIENTS | SERVES 6

2 tablespoons olive oil

1 large onion, diced

3 cloves garlic, minced

1 carrot, diced

1 parsnip, diced

1 stalk celery, diced

1 pound tempeh, crumbled

1½ cups Vegetable Broth (see Chapter 3)

½ teaspoon hot paprika

½ teaspoon crushed rosemary

1 tablespoon vegan Worcestershire sauce

½ teaspoon dried savory

⅛ teaspoon salt

¼ teaspoon freshly ground black pepper

1 tablespoon cornstarch and 1 tablespoon water, mixed (if necessary)

¼ cup minced fresh parsley

2¾ cups plain mashed potatoes

1. Place the olive oil in a large sauté pan over medium heat. Sauté the onions, garlic, carrots, parsnips, celery, and tempeh for about 5 minutes.

2. Place the mixture into a round 4-quart slow cooker. Add the broth, paprika, rosemary, Worcestershire sauce, savory, salt, and pepper. Stir.

3. Cook on low for 6–8 hours. If the meat mixture still looks very wet, create a slurry by mixing together 1 tablespoon cornstarch and 1 tablespoon water. Stir this into the slow cooker.

4. In a medium bowl, mash the parsley and potatoes using a potato masher. Spread on top of the tempeh mixture in the slow cooker.

5. Cover and cook on high for 30–60 minutes, or until the potatoes are warmed through.

PER SERVING Calories: 318 | Fat: 14 g | Protein: 17 g | Sodium: 315 mg | Fiber: 3 g | Carbohydrates: 35 g | Sugar: 3 g

Save Time in the Morning

Take a few minutes the night before cooking to cut up any vegetables you need for a recipe. Place them in an airtight container or plastic bag and refrigerate until morning. Measure any dried spices and place them in a small container on the counter until needed.

Italian Tempeh with Cannellini Beans

This is an incredibly simple one-dish meal that is packed with flavor.

INGREDIENTS | SERVES 4

1½ pound tempeh, sliced into 1" strips

28 ounces crushed tomatoes

1 head roasted garlic

1 onion, minced

2 tablespoons capers

2 teaspoons Italian-blend herbs

1 (15-ounce) can cannellini beans, drained and rinsed

1. Place the tempeh into a 4-quart slow cooker. Add the tomatoes, garlic, onions, capers, and Italian-blend herbs.

2. Cover and cook on low for 7–8 hours.

3. Add the cannellini beans 1 hour before serving and continue to cook on low for the remaining time.

PER SERVING Calories: 461 | Fat: 19 g | Protein: 38 g | Sodium: 462 mg | Fiber: 7.5 g | Carbohydrates: 42 g | Sugar: 6.5 g

Tempeh Braised in Sauerkraut

Sauerkraut is fermented cabbage easily found in grocery stores.
Or, you can make your own slow cooker version instead (see Chapter 7).

INGREDIENTS | SERVES 6

3 cups sauerkraut

½ tablespoon caraway seeds

1 tablespoon yellow mustard seeds

1 small onion, thinly sliced

2 tablespoons apple cider vinegar

1 pound tempeh, cut into 1½" cubes

1. Place the sauerkraut, caraway seeds, mustard seeds, onions, and vinegar into a 4- or 6-quart slow cooker. Stir to distribute all ingredients evenly.

2. Add the tempeh; toss.

3. Cover and cook for 3–4 hours on low.

PER SERVING Calories: 179 | Fat: 8.5 g | Protein: 15 g | Sodium: 416 mg | Fiber: 2.5 g | Carbohydrates: 12 g | Sugar: 2 g

Tempeh Tamale Pie

In a slight variation from the baked classic, this version of tamale pie features plump, moist cornmeal dumplings.

INGREDIENTS | SERVES 4

2 tablespoons olive oil

1 large onion, minced

1 pound tempeh, crumbled

1 jalapeño, minced

2 cloves garlic, minced

1 (15-ounce) can diced tomatoes

1 (10-ounce) can diced tomatoes with green chiles

1 (15-ounce) can dark red kidney beans, drained and rinsed

4 chipotle peppers in adobo, minced

½ teaspoon hot Mexican chili powder

⅔ cup 2% milk or unsweetened soymilk

2 tablespoons canola oil

2 teaspoons baking powder

½ cup cornmeal

½ teaspoon salt

1. In a large sauté pan over medium heat, add the olive oil. Sauté the onion, tempeh, jalapeño, and garlic for 5 minutes.

2. Pour the tempeh mixture into a 4-quart slow cooker. Add the tomatoes, tomatoes with green chilies, beans, chipotle, and chili powder.

3. Cover and cook on low for 8 hours.

4. In a medium bowl, mix the milk or soymilk, oil, baking powder, cornmeal, and salt. Drop in ¼-cup mounds in a single layer on top of the tempeh.

5. Cover, and cook on high for 20 minutes without lifting the lid. The dumplings will look fluffy and light when fully cooked.

PER SERVING Calories: 635 | Fat: 27 g | Protein: 36 g | Sodium: 689 mg | Fiber: 16 g | Carbohydrates: 67 g | Sugar: 9 g

Canned Versus Fresh Tomatoes

While fresh tomatoes are delicious, canned tomatoes are a better choice in some recipes because they have already been cooked. Skins and seeds have been removed from canned tomatoes, which is also a bonus when seeds and skin might detract from the dish. There is also reason to believe that canned tomatoes are better sources of cancer-preventing lycopene simply because they are cooked, and that one can of crushed tomatoes or sauce is the equivalent of dozens of fresh tomatoes.

Wild Rice and Tempeh

All this hearty dish needs is a side of steamed vegetables to make it a complete meal.

INGREDIENTS | SERVES 4

1 onion, sliced
4 ounces button mushrooms, minced
1 cup wild rice
½ pound tempeh, cut into 1½" cubes
1½ cups Vegetable Broth (see Chapter 3)

Place all ingredients in a 4-quart slow cooker and stir until just combined. Cover and cook on low heat for 8 hours.

PER SERVING Calories: 268 | Fat: 6.5 g | Protein: 17.5 g | Sodium: 297 mg | Fiber: 3.5 g | Carbohydrates: 38 g | Sugar: 2.5 g

CHAPTER 14

Desserts

Peanut Butter Cake

Serve this cake with a drizzling of chocolate sauce on top to make it a peanut butter cup cake.

INGREDIENTS | SERVES 8

1 cup all-purpose flour
1 cup sugar
1 teaspoon baking powder
½ teaspoon baking soda
¾ cup water
½ cup peanut butter
⅛ cup vegetable oil
1 teaspoon vanilla extract

1. In a medium bowl, mix all the dry ingredients.

2. In another medium bowl, mix all the wet ingredients.

3. Spray slow cooker with nonstick cooking oil.

4. Combine the dry and wet ingredients and then pour into a 4-quart slow cooker. Cover and cook on medium-high heat for 1–2 hours.

PER SERVING Calories: 281 | Fat: 11 g | Protein: 5.5 g | Sodium: 214 mg | Fiber: 1.5 g | Carbohydrates: 40 g | Sugar: 26.5 g

Poached Mixed Berries

Poached mixed berries are delicious on their own or served over a scoop of vanilla ice cream or soy ice cream.

INGREDIENTS | SERVES 8

½ cup blackberries
½ cup blueberries
½ cup strawberries, quartered
3 cups water
1 cup white sugar
1 lemon, juiced

Add all ingredients to a 4-quart slow cooker. Cover and cook on low heat for 3–4 hours.

PER SERVING Calories: 109 | Fat: 0.1 g | Protein: 0.3 g | Sodium: 3 mg | Fiber: 1 g | Carbohydrates: 28 g | Sugar: 26 g

Frozen Versus Fresh Berries

Frozen berries have a slightly different texture after they're defrosted than fresh berries do, but the texture works well in slow cooker recipes because of the long cooking time. Frozen berries allow you to use all types year round, and they're usually cheaper than fresh berries, too.

Coconut Rice Pudding

Rice pudding, also referred to as porridge, is eaten around the world in many different forms.

INGREDIENTS | SERVES 8

1 cup white rice
1 quart soymilk
½ cup butter or vegan margarine
⅛ cup shredded coconut
1 cup sugar
1 teaspoon cinnamon
¼ teaspoon salt

Add all ingredients to a 4-quart slow cooker. Cover and cook on low heat for 6 hours.

PER SERVING Calories: 357 | Fat: 14 g | Protein: 6 g | Sodium: 137 mg | Fiber: 1.5 g | Carbohydrates: 52 g | Sugar: 30 g

"Baked" Apples

Serve these lightly spiced apples as a simple dessert or a breakfast treat.

INGREDIENTS | SERVES 6

6 baking apples, cored and halved
½ cup water
1 cinnamon stick
1 knob peeled fresh ginger
1 vanilla bean

Baking with Apples

When baking or cooking, choose apples with firm flesh such as Granny Smith, Jonathan, McIntosh, Cortland, Pink Lady, Pippin, or Winesap. They will be able to hold up to low cooking times without turning to mush. Leaving the skin on adds fiber.

1. Place the apples in a single layer on the bottom of a 4- or 6-quart slow cooker. Add the water, cinnamon stick, ginger, and vanilla bean.

2. Cover and cook on low for 6–8 hours, or until the apples are tender and easily pierced with a fork.

3. Use a slotted spoon to remove the apples from the insert. Discard the cinnamon stick, ginger, vanilla bean, and water. Serve hot.

PER SERVING Calories: 77 | Fat: 0.2 g | Protein: 0.5 g | Sodium: 0.6 mg | Fiber: 3 g | Carbohydrates: 20 g | Sugar: 16 g

Carrot Cake

Ice this cake with cream cheese frosting or for a vegan topping, glaze the cake while it's still warm.

INGREDIENTS | SERVES 8

1½ cups all-purpose flour
½ teaspoon baking soda
1 teaspoon baking powder
¼ teaspoon salt
¾ teaspoon cinnamon
¼ teaspoon ground cloves
⅛ teaspoon freshly grated nutmeg
2 large eggs or 2 mashed bananas
¾ cup sugar
⅓ cup butter or vegan margarine
¼ cup water
1 cup carrots, grated
½ cup chopped walnuts

Carrot Cake Glaze

Repeatedly pierce the top of the cake with a fork. Add ½ cup lemon, orange, or unsweetened pineapple juice; 1 teaspoon freshly grated lemon or orange zest; and 1½ cups of sifted powdered sugar to a microwave-safe measuring cup and stir to combine. Microwave on high for 30 seconds. Stir and repeat until sugar is dissolved. Pour evenly over the cake.

1. In a mixing bowl, add the flour, baking soda, baking powder, salt, cinnamon, cloves, and nutmeg. Stir to combine.

2. In a food processor, add the eggs or bananas, sugar, and butter or margarine. Process to cream together. Scrape into the flour mixture.

3. Pour in the water and add the grated carrots to the mixing bowl. Stir and fold to combine all ingredients. Fold in the nuts.

4. Treat a 4-quart slow cooker with nonstick spray. Add the carrot cake batter and use a spatula to spread it evenly in the crock.

5. Cover and cook on low for 2 hours, or until cake is firm in the center.

PER SERVING Calories: 298 | Fat: 14 g | Protein: 5.5 g | Sodium: 242 mg | Fiber: 1.5 g | Carbohydrates: 40 g | Sugar: 20 g

Banana Bread

Oat bran adds extra fiber to this recipe, making it a heart-healthier bread.

INGREDIENTS | SERVES 8

1½ cups all-purpose flour

½ cup oat bran

¾ cup sugar

¼ teaspoon baking soda

2 teaspoons baking powder

½ teaspoon salt

3 ripe bananas, mashed

6 tablespoons butter or vegan margarine, softened

2 large eggs, beaten or 2 teaspoons cornstarch + 2 tablespoons warm water

¼ cup plain yogurt or vegan yogurt

1 teaspoon vanilla

1¼ cups walnuts

Spiced Banana Bread

For cinnamon-spiced banana bread, in Step 1 add 1 teaspoon of ground cinnamon and ¼ teaspoon each of ground cloves, ginger, allspice, and nutmeg to the flour.

1. Add the flour, oat bran, sugar, baking soda, baking powder, and salt to a mixing bowl. Stir to mix.

2. In a food processor, add the bananas, butter, eggs, yogurt (or the vegan alternatives for each) and vanilla. Pulse to cream together.

3. Add the walnuts and flour mixture to the food processor. Pulse to combine and chop the walnuts. Scrape down the sides of the container with a spatula and pulse until mixed.

4. Treat a 4-quart slow cooker with nonstick spray. Add the batter to the slow cooker, using a spatula to spread it evenly across the bottom of the crock.

5. Cover and cook on high for 3 hours, or until a toothpick inserted in the center of the bread comes out clean.

6. Allow to cool uncovered before removing it from the slow cooker.

PER SERVING Calories: 432 | Fat: 22 g | Protein: 8.5 g | Sodium: 332 mg | Fiber: 4 g | Carbohydrates: 54 g | Sugar: 25 g

Hot Fudge Fondue

Leftover hot fudge fondue can be stored in a covered container in the refrigerator for up to 3 weeks. Reheat to serve, whisking in additional cream if needed.

INGREDIENTS | YIELDS 4 CUPS

1 cup butter or vegan margarine

1 cup heavy cream or soymilk

½ cup light corn syrup

Pinch salt

16 ounces semisweet chocolate chips

1 tablespoon vanilla extract

1. Add the butter or margarine, cream or soymilk, corn syrup, and salt to a 4-quart slow cooker. Cover and cook on low for 1 hour.

2. Uncover and stir with a silicone-coated whisk or heatproof spatula; cover, and cook for another hour. Uncover and stir or whisk until the sugar is completely dissolved.

3. Add the chocolate chips and vanilla. Stir or whisk until the chocolate is completely melted and incorporated into the fondue. Reduce the heat to warm until ready to serve directly from the slow cooker.

PER SERVING (¼ CUP) Calories: 318 | Fat: 25 g | Protein: 1.5 g | Sodium: 16 mg | Fiber: 1.5 g | Carbohydrates: 26 g | Sugar: 18 g

Easy Applesauce

Homemade applesauce is easy to make and tastes much better than what you can get in the store. It freezes well, too, so you can make extra when apples are in season.

INGREDIENTS | YIELDS ABOUT 4 CUPS

10 medium apples, peeled, cored, and sliced

2 tablespoons fresh lemon juice

2 tablespoons water

6" cinnamon stick (optional)

Sugar, to taste (optional)

1. In a 4-quart slow cooker, add the apples, lemon juice, water, and cinnamon stick, if using. Stir to mix.

2. Cover and cook on low for 5 hours, or until the apples are soft and tender.

3. For chunky applesauce, mash the apples with a potato masher. For smooth applesauce, purée in a food processor or blender, use an immersion blender, or press through a food mill or large-mesh strainer.

4. While applesauce is still warm, add sugar to taste, if desired. Store covered in the refrigerator for up to 2 weeks, or freeze.

PER SERVING (1 CUP) Calories: 194 | Fat: 0.5 g | Protein: 1 g | Sodium: 1 mg | Fiber: 5 g | Carbohydrates: 50 g | Sugar: 40 g

Chocolate-Almond Fondue

Fruit is often used for enjoying dessert fondue, but you can also try dipping pretzels or dense yellow cake for a different flavor.

INGREDIENTS | SERVES 16

2 (14-ounce) packages semisweet chocolate chips
2 cups plain soymilk
½ cup butter or vegan margarine
½ cup almond pieces

Vegan Chocolate Chips

Most chocolate chips contain some dairy, but you can find nondairy chips in most grocery stores. One brand to try is Ghirardelli Semisweet Chocolate Chips.

1. Add all ingredients to a 4-quart slow cooker. Cover and cook on low heat for 1 hour.

2. Serve the fondue warm with fruits such as strawberries, pineapples, apples, and bananas.

PER SERVING Calories: 319 | Fat: 22 g | Protein: 3.5 g | Sodium: 22 mg | Fiber: 3.5 g | Carbohydrates: 34 g | Sugar: 28 g

Chocolate-Cinnamon Fondue

Cinnamon is most often used in the ground form, but whole cinnamon sticks can be used, too. Just be sure to remove them from the fondue before serving.

INGREDIENTS | SERVES 16

2 (14-ounce) packages semisweet chocolate chips
2 cups plain soymilk
½ cup butter or vegan margarine
1 tablespoon ground cinnamon

1. Add all ingredients to a 4-quart slow cooker. Cover and cook on low heat for 1 hour.

2. Serve the fondue warm with fruits such as strawberries, pineapples, apples, and bananas.

PER SERVING Calories: 302 | Fat: 21 g | Protein: 3 g | Sodium: 22 mg | Fiber: 3 g | Carbohydrates: 33 g | Sugar: 27 g

Bananas Foster

Bananas Foster is usually made from flambéed bananas served over vanilla ice cream, but as this recipes proves, the bananas can be made in a slow cooker, too.

INGREDIENTS | SERVES 8

1 cup dark corn syrup

⅛ cup rum

½ teaspoon vanilla extract

1 teaspoon cinnamon

¾ cup butter or vegan margarine

½ teaspoon salt

10 bananas, peeled and cut into bite-sized pieces

4 cups vanilla ice cream or vegan vanilla ice cream

1. In a medium bowl, stir in the corn syrup, rum, vanilla extract, cinnamon, butter, and salt.

2. Add mixture and bananas to a 4-quart slow cooker. Cover and cook on low heat for 1–2 hours. Serve over a scoop of ice cream.

PER SERVING Calories: 563 | Fat: 25 g | Protein: 4 g | Sodium: 235 mg | Fiber: 4.5 g | Carbohydrates: 83 g | Sugar: 44 g

Caramel Apples and Pears

Vegan caramels can be purchased online at www.AllisonsGourmet.com.

INGREDIENTS | SERVES 8

2 green apples, cored, peeled, and cut into wedges

2 pears, cored, peeled, and cut into wedges

1 (14-ounce) package of caramels

⅛ cup butter or vegan margarine

1 teaspoon cinnamon

½ cup apple juice

Add all ingredients to a 4-quart slow cooker. Cover and cook on low heat for 1–2 hours.

PER SERVING Calories: 269 | Fat: 3 g | Protein: 0.3 g | Sodium: 20 mg | Fiber: 2 g | Carbohydrates: 61 g | Sugar: 40 g

Chocolate Cake

This chocolate cake is a classic dessert prepared in a whole new way.

INGREDIENTS | SERVES 8

2 cups all-purpose flour

2 cups sugar

¾ cup unsweetened cocoa powder

1¾ teaspoons baking powder

1¾ teaspoons baking soda

1¼ cups 2% milk or soymilk

2 eggs or equivalent egg replacement

½ cup vegetable oil

1¼ cups water

1 cup vegan icing

Vegan Icing

Finding vegan icing is a cinch because big-name companies sell it in grocery stores around the country. Duncan Hines and Betty Crocker both sell a variety of vegan icings.

1. In a medium bowl, mix all the dry ingredients.

2. In another medium bowl, mix all the wet ingredients except the icing.

3. Spray a 4-quart slow cooker with nonstick cooking oil.

4. Combine the dry and wet ingredients and pour into the slow cooker.

5. Cover and cook on medium-high heat for 1–2 hours.

6. Remove cake from slow cooker and cover with icing.

PER SERVING Calories: 649 | Fat: 24 g | Protein: 8 g | Sodium: 496 mg | Fiber: 4 g | Carbohydrates: 107 g | Sugar: 75 g

Red Velvet Cake

Cream cheese or vegan cream cheese icing is the perfect topping for moist red velvet cake.

INGREDIENTS | SERVES 8

2 cups all-purpose flour
2 cups sugar
½ teaspoon salt
1¼ cups sugar
2 tablespoons cocoa powder
2 teaspoons red food coloring
½ cup vegetable oil
2 eggs or equivalent egg replacement
1 cup 2% milk or soymilk
1 tablespoon vinegar
1½ teaspoons vanilla extract
1 cup vegan icing

1. In a medium bowl, mix all the dry ingredients.

2. In another medium bowl, mix all the wet ingredients.

3. Spray slow cooker with nonstick cooking oil.

4. Combine all ingredients and pour into a 4-quart slow cooker. Cover and cook on medium-high heat for 1–2 hours.

5. Remove cake from slow cooker and cover with icing.

PER SERVING Calories: 649 | Fat: 16 g | Protein: 6 g | Sodium: 182 mg | Fiber: 1.5 g | Carbohydrates: 123 g | Sugar: 97 g

Chocolate Almond Bars

Save your dollar at the grocery store and make an entire batch of homemade candy bars.

INGREDIENTS | SERVES 16

2 (14-ounce) packages semisweet chocolate chips
2 cups almond pieces

Fun Shapes

Homemade candy bars make easy and budget-friendly holiday gifts, and making them in fun shapes is a festive touch. Spray the inside of a cookie cutter with nonstick spray, then lay it on top of the wax paper before dropping the chocolate on. Pour the chocolate into the cookie cutter and leave it in place until the chocolate is slightly firm.

1. Add all ingredients to a 4-quart slow cooker. Cover and cook on low heat for 1 hour, stirring every 15 minutes.

2. With a large spoon, scoop out the chocolate mixture and drop it onto wax paper. Allow to cool for 20–30 minutes.

PER SERVING Calories: 303 | Fat: 20.5 g | Protein: 4.5 g | Sodium: 5.5 mg | Fiber: 4.5 g | Carbohydrates: 34 g | Sugar: 27 g

Chocolate Coconut Bars

Shredded coconut sometimes comes sweetened, but if you'd like to cut the sugar in this treat, use unsweetened instead.

INGREDIENTS | SERVES 16

2 (14-ounce) packages semisweet chocolate chips
1 cup shredded coconut

1. Add all ingredients to a 4-quart slow cooker. Cover and cook on low heat for 1 hour, stirring every 15 minutes.

2. With a large spoon, scoop out the chocolate mixture and drop it onto wax paper. Allow to cool for 20–30 minutes.

PER SERVING Calories: 252 | Fat: 16 g | Protein: 2 g | Sodium: 6 mg | Fiber: 3 g | Carbohydrates: 32 g | Sugar: 27 g

White Chocolate–Macadamia Nut Bars

*White chocolate is made from cocoa butter, not cocoa solids,
which means it does not have the same nutritional benefits as dark chocolate.*

INGREDIENTS | SERVES 16

2 (14-ounce) packages white chocolate chips

1 cup Macadamia nut pieces

1. Add all ingredients to a 4-quart slow cooker. Cover and cook on low heat for 1 hour, stirring every 15 minutes.

2. With a large spoon, scoop out the white chocolate mixture and drop it onto wax paper. Allow to cool for 20–30 minutes.

PER SERVING Calories: 295 | Fat: 21 g | Protein: 3 g | Sodium: 6 mg | Fiber: 3.5 g | Carbohydrates: 32 g | Sugar: 27 g

Chocolate-Covered Pretzels

*To easily "dip" all of the pretzels at once, you can pour them all into the slow cooker, stir gently,
and pour the entire mixture into a colander to strain the excess chocolate.*

INGREDIENTS | SERVES 16

2 (14-ounce) packages semisweet chocolate chips

2 cups plain soymilk

½ cup butter or vegan margarine

4 cups miniature pretzels

1. Add all ingredients except pretzels to a 4-quart slow cooker. Cover, and cook on low heat for 1 hour.

2. Dip the pretzels in the chocolate and allow to cool on wax paper for 20–30 minutes.

PER SERVING Calories: 355 | Fat: 21 g | Protein: 4.5 g | Sodium: 211 mg | Fiber: 3.5 g | Carbohydrates: 44 g | Sugar: 28 g

Ginger Poached Pears

Fresh ginger best compliments pear flavor, but if you only have ground,
start by adding a smaller amount and then increasing after tasting.

INGREDIENTS | SERVES 8

5 pears, peeled, cored, and cut into wedges

3 cups water

1 cup white sugar

2 tablespoons ginger, minced

1 teaspoon cinnamon

Add all ingredients to a 4-quart slow cooker. Cover and cook on low heat for 4 hours.

PER SERVING Calories: 157 | Fat: 0 g | Protein: 0.5 g | Sodium: 1 mg | Fiber: 3 g | Carbohydrates: 41 g | Sugar: 35 g

Cinnamon Poached Apples

Red apples, such as Gala or red Delicious, compliment the cinnamon and ground ginger in this recipe.

INGREDIENTS | SERVES 8

5 apples, peeled, cored, and cut into wedges

3 cups water

1 cup white sugar

1 teaspoon ground ginger

1 teaspoon cinnamon

Add all ingredients to a 4-quart slow cooker. Cover and cook on low heat for 4 hours.

PER SERVING Calories: 145 | Fat: 0 g | Protein: 0.2 g | Sodium: 3 mg | Fiber: 2 g | Carbohydrates: 38 g | Sugar: 35 g

CHAPTER 15

Breakfast

Tofu Fritatta

Frittatas are traditionally made with eggs,
but you can use tofu instead for a cholesterol-free breakfast dish.

INGREDIENTS | SERVES 4

2 tablespoons olive oil

1 cup red potatoes, peeled and diced

½ onion, diced

½ cup red pepper, diced

½ cup green pepper, diced

1 teaspoon jalapeño, minced

1 clove garlic, minced

¼ cup parsley

16 ounces firm tofu

½ cup unsweetened soymilk

4 teaspoons cornstarch

2 tablespoons nutritional yeast

1 teaspoon mustard

½ teaspoon turmeric

1 teaspoon salt

¼ teaspoon black pepper

1. Add the oil to a 4-quart slow cooker and sauté the potatoes, onions, peppers, jalapeño, and garlic on low heat for about 15–20 minutes.

2. Meanwhile, in a blender or food processor, combine the rest of the ingredients until smooth, then pour the mixture into the slow cooker with the potatoes.

3. Cover and cook on medium-high heat for 4 hours, or until the frittata has firmed.

PER SERVING Calories: 243 | Fat: 12 g | Protein: 14 g | Sodium: 993 mg | Fiber: 5 g | Carbohydrates: 23 g | Sugar: 5 g

Make It a Scramble

To shorten the preparation time for this meal while keeping all of the flavors, try making this dish into a scramble by preparing the entire recipe in the slow cooker. Skip the step of blending the tofu and omit the cornstarch. Add remaining ingredients, breaking apart tofu as you stir, and sauté until cooked through.

Sunrise Tofu Scramble

Go gourmet with this tofu scramble by substituting shiitake mushrooms and Japanese eggplant instead of the broccoli and button mushrooms.

INGREDIENTS | SERVES 4

16 ounces firm tofu, drained and crumbled

½ cup broccoli florets, chopped

½ cup button mushrooms, sliced

2 tablespoons olive oil

2 teaspoons turmeric

1 teaspoon cumin

¼ teaspoon garlic powder

⅛ teaspoon red pepper flakes

2 cloves garlic, minced

1 teaspoon salt

¼ teaspoon black pepper

½ cup tomato, diced

1 lemon, juiced

2 tablespoons fresh parsley, chopped

1. Add the tofu, broccoli, mushrooms, oil, turmeric, cumin, garlic powder, red pepper flakes, garlic, salt, and black pepper to a 4-quart slow cooker. Cover and cook on medium heat for 4 hours.

2. Add the tomatoes, lemon juice, and parsley to the scramble and serve.

PER SERVING Calories: 146 | Fat: 10 g | Protein: 8.5 g | Sodium: 636 mg | Fiber: 1 g | Carbohydrates: 6 g | Sugar: 2.5 g

Country Grits

Start these simple grits in the evening and wake up to a delicious breakfast in the morning.

INGREDIENTS | SERVES 4

2 cups stone-ground grits

6 cups water

2 tablespoons butter or vegan margarine

1 teaspoon salt

¼ teaspoon black pepper

⅛ teaspoon cayenne pepper

Add all ingredients to a 4-quart slow cooker. Cover and cook on low heat for 6–9 hours.

PER SERVING Calories: 335 | Fat: 6.5 g | Protein: 7 g | Sodium: 591 mg | Fiber: 4 g | Carbohydrates: 65 g | Sugar: 1 g

Grits in the South

Grits—made from ground dried hominy (specially processed corn)—have many variations in the South. They are especially popular for breakfast, served in place of potatoes. A few of the most common ways to serve grits are with cheese, jam, butter, milk, or just plain.

Cheese Grits

*Top each individual bowl of grits with cheese and place
in the broiler until melted for an even tastier treat.*

INGREDIENTS | SERVES 4

2 cups stone-ground grits

6 cups water

2 tablespoons butter or vegan margarine

1 cup shredded Cheddar or vegan cheese

1 teaspoon salt

¼ teaspoon black pepper

⅛ teaspoon cayenne pepper

Add all ingredients to a 4-quart slow cooker. Cover and cook on low heat for 6–9 hours.

PER SERVING Calories: 449 | Fat: 16 g | Protein: 14 g | Sodium: 767 mg | Fiber: 4 g | Carbohydrates: 65 g | Sugar: 1 g

Almond and Dried Cherry Granola

Agave nectar is a natural sweetener that many vegans choose to use in place of honey.

INGREDIENTS | SERVES 24

5 cups old-fashioned rolled oats
1 cup slivered almonds
¼ cup agave nectar
¼ cup canola oil
1 teaspoon vanilla
½ cup dried tart cherries
¼ cup unsweetened flaked coconut
½ cup sunflower seeds

1. Place the oats and almonds into a 4-quart slow cooker. Drizzle with agave nectar, oil, and vanilla. Stir the mixture to distribute the syrup evenly.

2. Cook on high, uncovered, for 1½ hours, stirring every 15–20 minutes.

3. Add the cherries, coconut, and sunflower seeds. Reduce heat to low. Cook for 4 hours, uncovered, stirring every 20 minutes.

4. Allow the granola to cool fully, and then store it in an airtight container for up to 1 month.

PER SERVING Calories: 140 | Fat: 7 g | Protein: 4 g | Sodium: 1.5 mg | Fiber: 2.5 g | Carbohydrates: 16.5 g | Sugar: 3.5 g

Breakfast Quinoa with Fruit

Take a break from oatmeal and try this fruity quinoa instead!

INGREDIENTS | SERVES 4

1 cup quinoa

2 cups water

½ cup dried mixed berries

1 pear, thinly sliced

1 teaspoon dark brown sugar

½ teaspoon ground ginger

¼ teaspoon cinnamon

⅛ teaspoon cloves

⅛ teaspoon nutmeg

Place all ingredients into a 4-quart slow cooker. Cover and cook on low heat for 2–3 hours, or until the quinoa is fully cooked.

PER SERVING Calories: 231 | Fat: 3 g | Protein: 6 g | Sodium: 10 mg | Fiber: 5 g | Carbohydrates: 51 g | Sugar: 15 g

Quinoa

Quinoa, pronounced "keen-wah," is actually a seed, not a grain, closely related to spinach. It was originally cultivated by the Incas. It contains more high-quality protein than any other grain or cereal and is also high in iron, magnesium, phosphorous, and zinc, and a source of calcium, B vitamins, and fiber.

French Toast Casserole

This recipe is great for breakfast, and it's a wonderful way to use bread that is slightly stale.

INGREDIENTS | SERVES 8

12 slices whole-grain raisin bread

6 eggs

1 teaspoon vanilla

2 cups fat-free evaporated milk

2 tablespoons dark brown sugar

1 teaspoon cinnamon

¼ teaspoon nutmeg

Make It Vegan

To make this recipe vegan, leave out the eggs and evaporated milk. Instead, combine 2 teaspoons cornstarch with 2 tablespoons warm water and whisk until well combined. Add 1 cup soymilk to the cornstarch and stir again. Use this mixture in Step 2 of the recipe, and continue with the remaining steps as instructed.

1. Spray a 4-quart slow cooker with nonstick spray. Layer the bread in the slow cooker.

2. In a small bowl, whisk the eggs, vanilla, evaporated milk, brown sugar, cinnamon, and nutmeg. Pour over the bread.

3. Cover and cook on low for 6–8 hours.

4. Remove the lid and cook uncovered for 30 minutes, or until the liquid has evaporated.

PER SERVING Calories: 230 | Fat: 6 g | Protein: 13 g | Sodium: 280 mg | Fiber: 2 g | Carbohydrates: 32 g | Sugar: 12 g

Hash Browns

Also called home fries, this home-style dish will serve 4 as a main dish or 6 if part of a hearty breakfast.

INGREDIENTS | SERVES 4

1 teaspoon canola oil

1 large onion, thinly sliced

1½ pounds red skin potatoes, thinly sliced

1. Heat oil in a nonstick skillet. Add the onions and potatoes and sauté until just browned, about 6 minutes. The potatoes should not be fully cooked.

2. Add mixture to a 2- or 4-quart slow cooker. Cook on low for 3–4 hours or on high for 1½ hours.

PER SERVING Calories: 142 | Fat: 1.5 g | Protein: 3.5 g | Sodium: 12 mg | Fiber: 3.5 g | Carbohydrates: 30 g | Sugar: 3 g

Onion, Pepper, and Potato Hash

Use a cheese grater to grate the potatoes for this dish.

INGREDIENTS | SERVES 4

2 tablespoons olive oil

4 cups russet potatoes, peeled and grated

½ onion, diced

1 poblano pepper, cored and diced

2 cloves garlic, minced

1 teaspoon chili powder

½ teaspoon paprika

½ teaspoon cumin

1 teaspoon salt

¼ teaspoon pepper

Add all ingredients to a 4-quart slow cooker. Cover and cook on medium heat for 4 hours.

PER SERVING Calories: 190 | Fat: 7 g | Protein: 3.5 g | Sodium: 604 mg | Fiber: 2.5 g | Carbohydrates: 30 g | Sugar: 1.5 g

Better Hash Browns

After you have grated the potatoes for the hash browns, make sure to rinse them in a colander to get rid of the extra starch. Then, allow the potatoes to dry so they will get extra crispy in the slow cooker.

Pear Oatmeal

Cooking rolled oats overnight makes them so creamy they could be served as dessert.
Cooking them with fruit is just the icing on the cake.

INGREDIENTS | SERVES 4

2 Bosc pears, cored and thinly sliced

2¼ cups pear cider

1½ cups old-fashioned rolled oats

1 tablespoon dark brown sugar

½ teaspoon cinnamon

Place all ingredients in a 4-quart slow cooker. Cook on low overnight, approximately 8–9 hours. Stir and serve.

PER SERVING Calories: 220 | Fat: 2.5 g | Protein: 6 g | Sodium: 0 mg | Fiber: 7 g | Carbohydrates: 43 g | Sugar: 21 g

A Quick Guide to Oatmeal

Oat groats are oats that still have the bran, but the outer husk has been removed. Rolled oats are groats that have been rolled into flat flakes for quick cooking, a process that removes the bran. Scottish oats are oat groats that have been chopped to include the bran. Quick-cooking or instant oats are more processed rolled oats.

Tempeh Sausage Crumbles

Try this delicious and nutritious alternative to pork sausage.

INGREDIENTS | SERVES 4

1 (13-ounce) package tempeh, crumbled
1 teaspoon dried sage
2 teaspoons brown sugar
⅛ teaspoon red pepper flakes
⅛ teaspoon dried marjoram
1 cup vegetarian "chicken" broth
1 teaspoon salt
¼ teaspoon black pepper

1. In a medium bowl, mix all the ingredients together.

2. Add all ingredients to a 4-quart slow cooker. Cover and cook on medium heat for 4 hours.

PER SERVING Calories: 360 | Fat: 20 g | Protein: 33 g | Sodium: 606 mg | Fiber: 0 g | Carbohydrates: 19 g | Sugar: 2.5 g

Spicy Tofu Scramble

Serve this spicy scramble on it's own or rolled up in a flour tortilla to make a delicious breakfast burrito.

INGREDIENTS | SERVES 4

2 tablespoons olive oil

½ onion, diced

½ red pepper, diced

2 cloves garlic, minced

1 (16-ounce) package firm tofu, drained and crumbled

2 teaspoons turmeric

1 teaspoon cumin

½ teaspoon chipotle powder

½ teaspoon chili powder

1 teaspoon salt

¼ teaspoon black pepper

¼ cup tomato, diced

1 lemon, juiced

2 tablespoons fresh cilantro, chopped

1. Add the oil to a 4-quart slow cooker and sauté the onion, red pepper, and garlic on medium-high heat for about 3 minutes.

2. Mix in the tofu, turmeric, cumin, chipotle powder, chili powder, salt, and black pepper. Cover and cook on medium heat for 2–4 hours.

3. About 5 minutes before the scramble is finished, add the tomatoes, lemon juice, and cilantro.

PER SERVING Calories: 148 | Fat: 10 g | Protein: 8.5 g | Sodium: 635 mg | Fiber: 1 g | Carbohydrates: 6.5 g | Sugar: 2.5 g

Breakfast Scrambles

Some of the best scrambles are the ones that you do on the fly! Use the ingredients that you have in your fridge to create new and exciting dishes.

Breakfast Tofu and Veggies

Nutritional yeast has a cheesy flavor, and should not be replaced with other types of yeast.

INGREDIENTS | SERVES 4

¼ cup olive oil

1 (16-ounce) package extra-firm tofu, drained and cubed

½ onion, diced

1 cup broccoli, chopped

½ green bell pepper, chopped

½ zucchini, chopped

½ cup yellow squash, chopped

3 tablespoons soy sauce

¼ cup nutritional yeast

1. Add the oil to a 4-quart slow cooker and sauté the tofu for about 5–8 minutes on medium high heat, stirring occasionally.

2. Add the vegetables and the soy sauce. Cover and cook on medium heat for 2–4 hours.

3. About 1 minute before the tofu and veggies are finished, stir in the nutritional yeast and serve.

PER SERVING Calories: 300 | Fat: 18 g | Protein: 23 g | Sodium: 1,473 mg | Fiber: 2.5 g | Carbohydrates: 12 g | Sugar: 5 g

Easy Tofu "Eggs"

Tofu "eggs" are a great form of protein and taste delicious. They contain very little fat and no cholesterol. Build upon this basic recipe to create a variety of tofu scrambles.

INGREDIENTS | SERVES 4

2 tablespoons olive oil

1 (16-ounce) package firm tofu, drained and crumbled

¼ cup onion, diced

2 cloves garlic, minced

1 teaspoon turmeric

1 teaspoon salt

¼ teaspoon black pepper

1 lemon, juiced

1. Add all ingredients, except for the lemon juice, to a 4-quart slow cooker. Cover and cook on medium heat for 2–4 hours.

2. About 3 minutes before the "eggs" are finished, stir in the lemon juice.

PER SERVING Calories: 137 | Fat: 9.5 g | Protein: 8 g | Sodium: 630 mg | Fiber: 0.5 g | Carbohydrates: 4.5 g | Sugar: 2 g

Grandma's Cornmeal Mush

This recipe cooks into a thick cornmeal porridge. It makes for a tasty and inexpensive breakfast food.

INGREDIENTS | SERVES 4

2 cups yellow cornmeal

8 cups water

1 teaspoon salt

2 tablespoons butter or vegan margarine

1. Add all ingredients to a 4-quart slow cooker. Cover and cook on medium heat for 4 hours.

2. Allow the mush to cool for at least 30 minutes. Serve with maple syrup.

PER SERVING Calories: 305 | Fat: 7 g | Protein: 5 g | Sodium: 609 mg | Fiber: 2.5 g | Carbohydrates: 54 g | Sugar: 1 g

Breakfast Casserole

To simplify this recipe, use Morningstar Farm Sausage Style Crumbles instead of the recipe in this book. Omit the cottage cheese to make this a vegan dish.

INGREDIENTS | SERVES 4

¼ cup olive oil

3 cups potatoes, peeled and grated

1 onion, diced

½ green bell pepper, chopped

2 cups Tempeh Sausage Crumbles (see recipe in this chapter)

6 eggs, beaten or Easy Tofu "Eggs" (see recipe in this chapter)

1 cup cottage cheese

2 cups Cheddar cheese or vegan cheese

1 teaspoon salt

¼ teaspoon black pepper

Add all ingredients to a 4-quart slow cooker. Cover and cook on medium heat for 4 hours.

PER SERVING Calories: 757 | Fat: 51 g | Protein: 47 g | Sodium: 1,252 mg | Fiber: 3.5 g | Carbohydrates: 31 g | Sugar: 5 g

Spicy Breakfast Burrito

To make this burrito vegetarian instead of vegan, use cooked eggs instead of tofu.

INGREDIENTS | SERVES 4

¼ cup olive oil

1 (16-ounce) package firm tofu, drained and crumbled

¼ cup red onion, diced

1 tablespoon jalapeño, minced

¼ cup red bell pepper, diced

¼ cup poblano pepper, diced

1 cup cooked black beans, drained

2 teaspoons turmeric

1 teaspoon cumin

½ teaspoon chili powder

1 teaspoon salt

¼ teaspoon black pepper

4 large flour tortillas

1 avocado, peeled and sliced

½ cup tomatoes, diced

¼ cup cilantro, chopped

½ cup chipotle salsa

½ cup shredded Cheddar cheese or vegan Cheddar cheese

1. Add olive oil, tofu, onion, jalapeño, red bell pepper, and poblano pepper to a 4-quart slow cooker and sauté on medium-high for 5–8 minutes.

2. Add the black beans, turmeric, cumin, chili powder, salt, and black pepper. Cover and cook on medium heat for 4 hours.

3. Scoop the filling onto the tortillas and add the avocado, tomato, cilantro, salsa, and cheese. Fold the sides of the tortilla in and roll up the burrito.

PER SERVING Calories: 499 | Fat: 29 g | Protein: 23 g | Sodium: 1,088 mg | Fiber: 9.5 g | Carbohydrates: 37 g | Sugar: 5 g

Steaming Tortillas

For best results, steam tortillas on the stovetop using a steamer basket. If you're in a hurry, throw the tortillas into the microwave one at a time and heat for about 30 seconds.

Tofu Ranchero

Bring Mexican cuisine to the breakfast table with an easy tofu ranchero.

INGREDIENTS | SERVES 4

3 tablespoons olive oil

1 (16-ounce) package firm tofu, drained and crumbled

½ onion, diced

2 cloves garlic, minced

1 lemon, juiced

½ teaspoon turmeric

1 teaspoon salt

¼ teaspoon black pepper

1 cup pinto beans, drained

8 corn tortillas

½ cup shredded Cheddar cheese or vegan Cheddar cheese

½ cup chipotle salsa

1. Add the olive oil, tofu, onion, garlic, lemon, turmeric, salt, black pepper, and pinto beans to a 4-quart slow cooker. Cover and cook on medium heat for 4 hours.

2. When the ranchero filling is nearly done, brown the tortillas on both sides using a small sauté pan.

3. Preheat the oven to 350°F.

4. Place the tortillas on a baking sheet and add the filling. Sprinkle the cheese over of the rancheros and bake until the cheese has melted, about 5 minutes. Top with the chipotle salsa.

PER SERVING Calories: 472 | Fat: 23 g | Protein: 25 g | Sodium: 960 mg | Fiber: 7 g | Carbohydrates: 43 g | Sugar: 4.5 g

Choosing Salsa

Salsa comes in many delicious and unique varieties. Most are clearly labeled mild, medium, and hot, but one's interpretation of those words can vary greatly. Chipotle salsa has a deep, earthy spice, but you can also use plain tomato salsa or tomatillo salsa in this recipe.

Rosemary Home Fries

Like hash browns, home fries can also be served with a variety of toppings or plain with a side of ketchup.

INGREDIENTS | SERVES 4

¼ cup olive oil

4 cups red potatoes, diced

½ red onion, diced

1 poblano pepper, diced

½ red bell pepper, diced

1 teaspoon salt

¼ teaspoon black pepper

2 tablespoon fresh rosemary, chopped

1. Add all ingredients, except for the rosemary, to a 4-quart slow cooker. Cover and cook on medium heat for 4 hours.

2. About 10 minutes before the potatoes are done, add the rosemary and cook for the remainder of the time.

PER SERVING Calories: 234 | Fat: 13.5 g | Protein: 3 g | Sodium: 599 mg | Fiber: 3 g | Carbohydrates: 26 g | Sugar: 2.5 g

White Gravy

For a delicious and filling breakfast, try this gravy over biscuits.

INGREDIENTS | SERVES 4

½ cup vegetable oil

¼ cup onion, minced

3 cloves garlic, minced

¼ cup flour

4 tablespoons soy sauce

2 cups water

½ teaspoon dried sage

⅛ teaspoon dried thyme

½ teaspoon salt

¼ teaspoon black pepper

1. Add the oil to the slow cooker and sauté the onion and garlic over medium heat for about 3–5 minutes. Slowly stir in the flour to create a roux.

2. Add the rest of the ingredients to the slow cooker. Cover and cook on medium heat for 1 hour, stirring occasionally.

PER SERVING Calories: 285 | Fat: 27 g | Protein: 2 g | Sodium: 1,197 mg | Fiber: 0.5 g | Carbohydrates: 9 g | Sugar: 0 g

CHAPTER 16

Beverages

Hot Cranberry-Pineapple Punch

If you prefer, you can omit the brown sugar and water called for in this recipe and sweeten it with 2 cups of apple juice instead.

INGREDIENTS | SERVES 20

8 cups cranberry juice

8 cups unsweetened pineapple juice

2 cups brown sugar, packed

2 cups water

2 (3") cinnamon sticks

2 teaspoons whole cloves

Chilled Cranberry-Pineapple Punch

After slow cooking, allow the punch to cool to room temperature and then chill until needed. Add 3–4 cups lemon-lime soda or Mountain Dew. Serve in punch cups or in tall glasses over ice, garnished with a maraschino cherry.

1. In a 4-quart slow cooker, add the cranberry juice, pineapple juice, brown sugar, and water.

2. Break the cinnamon sticks into smaller pieces and add them along with the whole cloves to a muslin spice bag or wrap them in cheesecloth tied shut with cotton string or kitchen twine. Add to the slow cooker.

3. Cover and cook on low for 1 hour.

4. Uncover and stir until the brown sugar is dissolved into the juice.

5. Cover and cook for another 7–8 hours.

6. Uncover the cooker and remove the spice bag or cheesecloth; holding over the slow cooker, squeeze to extract the seasoned juice. To serve, ladle into heatproof mugs.

PER SERVING Calories: 183 | Fat: 0.2 g | Protein: 0.5 g | Sodium: 10 mg | Fiber: 0.3 g | Carbohydrates: 46 g | Sugar: 43 g

Ginger-Pear Punch

Adding a touch of sparkling water at the end will make this punch even more refreshing.

INGREDIENTS | SERVES 6 6 cups water ½ cup sugar 1" piece fresh ginger, peeled and grated 6 pears, peeled and diced Ice 24 ounces sparkling water	1. In a 4-quart slow cooker, add the water, sugar, and ginger. 2. Place the pear in a cheesecloth and twist to close, then add to the slow cooker. 3. Cover and cook on low heat for 3 hours. 4. Allow the punch to cool completely, then fill each glass with ice, ¾ full with the punch, then top it off with a splash of plain sparkling water.

PER SERVING Calories: 162 | Fat: 0.2 g | Protein: 0.5 g | Sodium: 2 mg | Fiber: 5 g | Carbohydrates: 42 g | Sugar: 33 g

White Tea–Berry Fusion

Fruit-filled teas are delicious served warm or chilled and served over ice.

INGREDIENTS | SERVES 8

8 white tea bags
½ cup blackberries, halved
½ cup raspberries, halved
2 tablespoons sugar
8 cups water

1. Add all ingredients to a 4-quart slow cooker. Cover and cook on low heat for 2 hours.

2. Remove the tea bags and strain the fruit before serving.

PER SERVING Calories: 22 | Fat: 0 g | Protein: 0.4 g | Sodium: 9 mg | Fiber: 1 g | Carbohydrates: 5 g | Sugar: 3 g

White Tea

White tea is harvested mainly in China. It is made from immature tea leaves plucked just before the buds fully open. The leaves go through even less processing than green tea leaves (they are steamed rather than air dried). Because of this, they remain close to their natural state, meaning they contain more cancer-fighting polyphenols than other teas. White tea has also been found to bolster the immune system and prevent plaque.

Vanilla-Lavender Tea

Black tea, green tea, or white tea will all work well in this recipe. The choice is yours!

INGREDIENTS | SERVES 8

8 black tea bags
8 cups water
½ teaspoon vanilla extract
1 tablespoon sugar
2 sprigs lavender

1. Place the tea bags, water, vanilla extract, and sugar in a 4-quart slow cooker.

2. Place the lavender in a cheese cloth and twist to close, then add to the slow cooker.

3. Cover and cook on low heat for 2 hours.

4. Remove the tea bags and lavender before serving the tea warm.

PER SERVING Calories: 7 | Fat: 0 g | Protein: 0 g | Sodium: 7 mg | Fiber: 0 g | Carbohydrates: 1.5 g | Sugar: 1.5 g

Chai Tea

Chai tea typically refers to tea that has been brewed with Indian spices and herbs.

INGREDIENTS | SERVES 8

8 bags Darjeeling tea

2 quarts water

1 cinnamon stick

8 whole cloves

1 cup soymilk

2 tablespoons sugar

5 cardamom pods

1 tablespoon fresh ginger, sliced

1. Place the tea bags, water, cinnamon, cloves, soymilk, sugar, cardamom, and ginger in a 4-quart slow cooker. Cover and cook on low heat for 2 hours.

2. Pour the tea through a strainer and serve warm.

PER SERVING Calories: 35 | Fat: 0.5 g | Protein: 1 g | Sodium: 15 mg | Fiber: 0.5 g | Carbohydrates: 5 g | Sugar: 4 g

Iced Chai

Chai tea can be enjoyed warm during the winter or cold in the summer. Simply pour the chai over ice or combine a glass of tea with a ½–1 cup of ice in the blender.

Café Mocha

*With many drinks at specialty coffee shops coming in around $5,
you can save big money by making a budget-friendly version at home.*

INGREDIENTS | SERVES 12

8 cups fresh-brewed coffee

2 cups 2% milk or soymilk

4 tablespoons chocolate sauce

2 ounces dark chocolate, finely chopped

Coffee in America

Coffee consumption is on the rise in the United States. Studies show that Americans now drink a whopping 336 million cups of coffee each year!

1. Add all the ingredients in a 4-quart slow cooker. Cover and cook on low heat for 2 hours.

2. Serve warm or chilled and top with whipped cream if desired.

PER SERVING Calories: 63 | Fat: 2 g | Protein: 2 g | Sodium: 29 mg | Fiber: 0.5 g | Carbohydrates: 0.5 g | Sugar: 7 g

Pumpkin Spice

Canned pumpkin works in this recipe as long as the texture is very smooth.

INGREDIENTS | SERVES 8

1 cup puréed pumpkin

8 cups 2% milk or soymilk

2 tablespoons sugar

½ teaspoon ground cloves

½ teaspoon allspice

½ teaspoon ground cinnamon

Add all ingredients to a 4-quart slow cooker and stir until very well combined. Cover and cook on low heat for 2 hours.

PER SERVING Calories: 147 | Fat: 4 g | Protein: 8 g | Sodium: 124 mg | Fiber: 1.5 g | Carbohydrates: 19 g | Sugar: 13 g

Minty Hot Chocolate

Several brands of chocolate syrup such as Hershey's are "accidentally vegan."
Just be sure to read the label before purchasing.

INGREDIENTS | SERVES 8

8 cups 2% milk or soymilk
8 tablespoons chocolate syrup
¼ cup fresh mint, chopped

Many Uses of Mint

Besides being a refreshing herb, mint has had many medicinal uses throughout history. It has been used to relieve headaches, cure indigestion and heartburn, and help people fall asleep.

1. Pour the milk or soymilk and chocolate syrup into a 4-quart slow cooker and stir well.

2. Place the fresh mint in a cheesecloth and twist until closed, then add to the slow cooker.

3. Cover and cook on low heat for 1 hour.

4. Remove the mint before serving warm.

PER SERVING Calories: 185 | Fat: 4.5 g | Protein: 8 g | Sodium: 137 mg | Fiber: 2 g | Carbohydrates: 28 g | Sugar: 19 g

Hot Buttered Rum

Time the cooking of this drink so that you can stir in the rum and let it mull for 20 minutes before serving.

INGREDIENTS | SERVES 12

½ cup unsalted butter or vegan margarine
8 cups water
2 cups firmly packed light brown sugar
Pinch salt
½ teaspoon freshly ground nutmeg
⅛ teaspoon ground cloves
⅛ teaspoon ground cinnamon
1 cup dark rum

1. Add the butter or margarine and 2 cups of the water to a 4-quart slow cooker. Cover and cook on high for ½ hour, or until the butter is melted.

2. Stir in the brown sugar, and then add the remaining water, salt, nutmeg, cloves, and cinnamon. Cover and cook on low for 2–4 hours.

3. Twenty minutes before serving, stir in the rum; cover, and cook for 20 minutes. To serve, ladle into small heatproof mugs.

PER SERVING Calories: 249 | Fat: 7.5 g | Protein: 0.1 g | Sodium: 11 mg | Fiber: 0 g | Carbohydrates: 36 g | Sugar: 35 g

Hot Toddy

Hot Toddies have been used for many years as an alternative remedy for congestion and colds.

INGREDIENTS | SERVES 8

½ cup bourbon
¼ cup honey
2 lemons, juiced
2 cups water
1 stick cinnamon

1. Add all ingredients to a 4-quart slow cooker and stir until very well combined. Cover and cook on low heat for 2 hours.

2. Remove the cinnamon stick and serve warm.

PER SERVING Calories: 71 | Fat: 0 g | Protein: 0.2 g | Sodium: 1 mg | Fiber: 0.5 g | Carbohydrates: 10 g | Sugar: 9 g

Origins of the Hot Toddy

The Hot Toddy originated in Scotland. Interestingly, the original version did not contain alcohol; that was added later for the medicinal value.

Spiked Apple Cider

The dark rum adds a delicious complexity to this cider.

INGREDIENTS | SERVES 6

6 cups apple cider
6 ounces dark rum
1 apple, cored and thinly sliced

Add all ingredients to a 4-quart slow cooker. Cover and cook on low heat for 2 hours.

PER SERVING Calories: 191 | Fat: 0.5 g | Protein: 0.3 g | Sodium: 10 mg | Fiber: 1 g | Carbohydrates: 31 g | Sugar: 26 g

Spiced Wine

This is a great wine to make for winter holiday parties.

INGREDIENTS | SERVES 6

1 (750-ml) bottle red wine
½ teaspoon ground cinnamon
½ teaspoon ground cloves
½ teaspoon ground nutmeg
1 tablespoon orange zest

Garnishments

After zesting your orange peel for the spiced wine, cut the orange into thin circles and add to each drink as a garnish. Alternatively, you may cut each orange wedge into 3 pieces and add to the slow cooker for increased fruity flavor.

Add all ingredients to a 4-quart slow cooker. Cover and cook on low heat for 2 hours.

PER SERVING Calories: 105 | Fat: 0 g | Protein: 0 g | Sodium: 5 mg | Fiber: 0 g | Carbohydrates: 3.5 g | Sugar: 1 g

Irish Coffee

The coffee, which is best made using medium-roast beans, can be made ahead and added to the slow cooker 2 hours before you plan to serve dessert.

INGREDIENTS | SERVES 16

16 cups coffee
½ cup sugar
1 cup Irish whiskey

Origins of Irish Coffee

Joseph Sheridan, a chef in Ireland, is said to be the first to ever serve Irish coffee. The drink was created to cheer up a group of American travelers on a gloomy, winter night in the 1940s.

1. If you are using chilled coffee, add it to a 4-quart slow cooker; cover, and cook on low for 1 hour. If you're using fresh-brewed coffee, you can skip this step.

2. Stir in the sugar until it's dissolved. Cover and cook on low for 1 hour.

3. To serve, ladle into heatproof mugs. Add whiskey and garnish with a dollop of whipped cream, if desired.

PER SERVING Calories: 61 | Fat: 0 g | Protein: 0.3 g | Sodium: 5 mg | Fiber: 0 g | Carbohydrates: 6 g | Sugar: 6 g

Mixed Berry Punch

Feel free to use whatever berries happen to be in season to create this refreshing punch.

INGREDIENTS | SERVES 8

1 cup blackberries
1 cup blueberries
1 cup strawberries
1 lemon, juiced
½ cup sugar
2 quarts water

1. Add all ingredients to a 4-quart slow cooker. Cover and cook on low heat for 2 hours.

2. Pour punch through a strainer and serve chilled.

PER SERVING Calories: 75 | Fat: 0.2 g | Protein: 0.6 g | Sodium: 1 mg | Fiber: 2 g | Carbohydrates: 19 g | Sugar: 16 g

Peach Iced Tea

If fresh peaches are not in season, use canned peaches instead.

INGREDIENTS | SERVES 8

8 bags black tea
2 quarts water
2 peaches, thinly sliced
½ cup sugar
4 whole cloves

1. Add all ingredients to a 4-quart slow cooker. Cover and cook on low heat for 2 hours.

2. Pour tea through a strainer and serve chilled.

PER SERVING Calories: 65 | Fat: 0 g | Protein: 0.3 g | Sodium: 7 mg | Fiber: 0.5 g | Carbohydrates: 17 g | Sugar: 15 g

Southern-Style Sweet Tea

Mix 4 ounces of sweet tea with 4 ounces of lemonade to create the famous Arnold Palmer drink.

INGREDIENTS | SERVES 8

8 bags black tea
2 quarts water
¾ cup sugar

Add all ingredients to a 4-quart slow cooker. Cover and cook on low heat for 2 hours.

PER SERVING Calories: 75 | Fat: 0 g | Protein: 0 g |
Sodium: 14 mg | Fiber: 0 g | Carbohydrates: 20 g | Sugar: 19 g

Sweet Tea History

Most sweet tea consumed in America before WWII was made with green tea. During the war, green tea sources were cut off, causing the United States to switch to black.

Mango-Mint Iced Tea

The sweetness of the mango combined with the refreshing bite of mint make this a must-have summer drink.

INGREDIENTS | SERVES 8

1 (15-ounce) can mangos, chopped
8 bags black tea
2 quarts water
¾ cup sugar
¼ cup mint leaves, whole

1. Add all ingredients to a 4-quart slow cooker. Cover and cook on low heat for 2 hours.

2. Pour tea through a strainer and serve chilled.

PER SERVING Calories: 111 | Fat: 0 g | Protein: 0.5 g |
Sodium: 11 mg | Fiber: 1 g | Carbohydrates: 29 g | Sugar: 27 g

Sangria

Sangria is a very common wine punch that originated in Spain.

INGREDIENTS | SERVES 8

1 (750-milliliter) bottle red wine
1 orange, halved
1 lime, halved
1 cup cherries
1 cup diced pineapples
½ cup brandy
1 quart ginger ale

1. Add all ingredients, except for the ginger ale, to a 4-quart slow cooker. Cover and cook on low heat for 2 hours.

2. Allow sangria to cool in the refrigerator for at least 1 hour. Add the ginger ale just before serving.

PER SERVING Calories: 181 | Fat: 0 g | Protein: 0.5 g | Sodium: 12 mg | Fiber: 1 g | Carbohydrates: 21 g | Sugar: 17 g

Honey-Mint Green Tea

Make this tea vegan by simply using sugar or agave nectar instead of honey.

INGREDIENTS | SERVES 8

8 bags green tea
2 quarts water
½ cup sugar
¼ cup honey
¼ cup mint leaves, whole

1. Add all ingredients to a 4-quart slow cooker. Cover and cook on low heat for 2 hours.

2. Pour tea through a strainer and serve warm or chilled.

PER SERVING Calories: 85 | Fat: 0 g | Protein: 0.1 g | Sodium: 10 mg | Fiber: 0.3 g | Carbohydrates: 22 g | Sugar: 21 g

Blackberry-Mint White Tea

The blackberries in this recipe can easily be exchanged for raspberries or blueberries.

INGREDIENTS | SERVES 8

8 bags white or green tea
2 quarts water
2 cups blackberries
¼ cup mint leaves, whole
¾ cup sugar

1. Add all ingredients to a 4-quart slow cooker. Cover and cook on low heat for 2 hours.

2. Pour tea through a strainer and serve warm or chilled.

PER SERVING Calories: 93 | Fat: 0.2 g | Protein: 0.5 g | Sodium: 10 mg | Fiber: 2 g | Carbohydrates: 23 g | Sugar: 20 g

Cherry and Lime Punch

Create a cherry and lime slushy by adding this punch and 3 cups ice to a blender.

INGREDIENTS | SERVES 8

2 cups frozen cherries
5 limes, halved
2 quarts water
½ cup sugar

1. Add all ingredients to a 4-quart slow cooker. Cover and cook on low heat for 2 hours.

2. Pour punch through a strainer and serve chilled.

PER SERVING Calories: 85 | Fat: 0.2 g | Protein: 0.7 g | Sodium: 8 mg | Fiber: 2 g | Carbohydrates: 23 g | Sugar: 18 g

Raspberry Lemonade

Raspberries are usually in season June through August, making this a great summer drink.

INGREDIENTS | SERVES 8

1 cup raspberries
10 lemons, juiced
½ cup sugar
2 quarts water

1. Add all ingredients to a 4-quart slow cooker. Cover and cook on low heat for 2 hours.

2. Pour lemonade through a strainer and serve chilled.

PER SERVING Calories: 77 | Fat: 0.3 g | Protein: 1 g | Sodium: 2 mg | Fiber: 1 g | Carbohydrates: 21 g | Sugar: 15 g

Cherry Lemonade

Cherries are very high in disease-fighting antioxidants.

INGREDIENTS | SERVES 8

2 cups frozen cherries
10 lemons, juiced
½ cup sugar
2 quarts water

1. Add all ingredients to a 4-quart slow cooker. Cover and cook on low heat for 2 hours.

2. Pour lemonade through a strainer and serve chilled.

PER SERVING Calories: 98 | Fat: 0.5 g | Protein: 1 g | Sodium: 32 mg | Fiber: 1 g | Carbohydrates: 26 g | Sugar: 19 g

Orange and Lime Punch

Use fresh-squeezed orange juice for an even tastier punch.

INGREDIENTS | SERVES 6

2 cups orange juice
5 limes, halved
½ cup sugar
2 quarts water

1. Add all ingredients to a 4-quart slow cooker. Cover and cook on low heat for 2 hours.

2. Pour punch through a strainer and serve chilled.

   PER SERVING Calories: 122 | Fat: 0.2 g | Protein: 1 g | Sodium: 3 mg | Fiber: 2 g | Carbohydrates: 32 g | Sugar: 24 g

Passion Fruit Green Tea

The passion fruit is native to Brazil and Argentina.

INGREDIENTS | SERVES 8

8 bags green tea
2 quarts water
½ cup sugar
½ passion fruit juice or nectar

1. Add all ingredients to a 4-quart slow cooker. Cover and cook on low heat for 2 hours.

2. Pour tea through a strainer and serve chilled.

   PER SERVING Calories: 79 | Fat: 0.2 g | Protein: 0.5 g | Sodium: 15 mg | Fiber: 3 g | Carbohydrates: 20 g | Sugar: 15 g

Glossary of Terms and Ingredients

Braising
A cooking method that consists of browning a protein or vegetable and then simmering it in liquid to finish it.

Caponata
A popular Italian dish made with eggplant and tomato.

Coulis
A sauce consisting of puréed vegetables or fruits.

Lemongrass
A thick, lemon-scented grass often used in Thai cooking.

Masala
An Indian curry that often includes cardamom, coriander, pepper, fennel, and nutmeg.

Orzo
A rice-shaped pasta.

Paella
A Spanish rice dish seasoned with saffron.

Quinoa
A tiny grain, similar to couscous, high in protein and nutrients.

Ratatouille
A vegetable stew often consisting of tomatoes, bell peppers, zucchini, squash, and onions.

Risotto
An Italian dish prepared by slowly stirring hot stock into rice.

Sauté
To fry briefly with a small amount of fat over high heat.

Seitan
A meat substitute made from wheat gluten.

Tempeh
An Indonesian food made from fermented soybeans and fungus.

Tofu
A cheese-like food made from soybeans.

TVP
Texturized vegetable protein, a meat substitute, similar to ground beef, made from soybeans.

Substitutions

Bacon
Soy bacon pieces such as Bacos or tempeh bacon

Butter
Nondairy vegan margarine such as Earth Balance

Buttermilk
Combine 1 cup soymilk with 1 tablespoon vinegar

Cheese
Rice milk, soymilk, or nondairy cheese such as Daiya or Follow Your Heart

Chicken stock
Vegetable stock or faux chicken stock such as Better Than Bouillon No Chicken Base

Cream cheese
Nondairy cream cheese such as Toffuti Better Than Cream Cheese or Vegan Gourmet Cream Cheese Alternative

Eggs
Ener-G Egg Replacer, cornstarch (2 teaspoons cornstarch plus 2 tablespoons warm water equals 1 egg), mashed banana (1 banana equals 1 egg), tofu, ground flax seed (1 tablespoon of ground flax seed plus 3 tablespoons hot water equals 1 egg)

Gelatin
Agar

Ground beef
Texturized vegetable protein (TVP) or soy beef such as Gimme Lean Beef or Boca Ground Crumbles

Heavy cream
Soy cream such as Silk Original Creamer or MimicCream Cream Subsitute

Honey
Agave nectar, maple syrup, or brown rice syrup

Ice cream
Soy ice cream such as Tofutti or Purely Decadent or coconut milk ice cream such as Purely Decadent Made With Coconut Milk

Marshmallows
Gelatin-free marshmallows such as Sweet and Sara

Milk
Sweetened or unsweetened soymilk, almond milk, or rice milk

Pork
Vegan Ground Pork by Match, Lightlife's Smart Bacon, or Smart Deli Baked Ham Style

Ricotta cheese
Crumbled firm tofu

Sausage
Meat-free sausage links such as Tofurky Kielbasa,
Beer Brats, or Sweet Italian

Sour cream
Nondairy sour cream such as Vegan Gourmet
Sour Cream Alternative or Tofutti Sour Supreme

Whipped cream
Soy whipped cream such as Soyatoo Soy Whip

Yogurt
Soy yogurt such as Silk Live! Soy Yogurt or coco-
nut milk yogurt such as So Delicious Coconut
Milk Yogurt

Internet Resources

Vegetarian/Vegan Information

PETA.org

A comprehensive resource provided by the world's largest animal rights group. Contains information on animal rights, a free vegetarian starter kit, vegan recipes, cruelty-free shopping guide, "accidentally vegan" shopping list, games, contests, celebrity ads, and more.

www.peta.org

Vegan Online Stores

Cosmo's Vegan Shoppe

100% vegan specialty store based in Atlanta, Georgia. Sells food, clothing, home products, cosmetics, media, and beauty and healthcare products.

www.cosmosveganshoppe.com

The Vegan Store

The first vegan store that started as a mail-order catalog and is now online. Sells food, clothing, home products, cosmetics, media, and beauty and healthcare products.

www.veganstore.com

Food Fight! Vegan Grocery

A Portland, Oregon–based vegan food store. Sells vegan meats, cheeses, sweets, beverages, and vitamins.

www.foodfightgrocery.com

Recipes

PETA.org

Free vegan recipes for breakfast, lunch, dinner, dessert, and snacks, covering almost all global cuisines.

www.peta.org

VegWeb.com

Over 13,000 vegetarian recipes and photos provided by registered users. The site also contains forums, a meal planner, articles, and coupons.

www.vegweb.com

Fat-Free Vegan Recipes

Low-fat and no-fat vegan recipes. The site also contains a popular blog, forum, and additional information on fat-free cooking.

www.fatfreevegan.com

Post Punk Kitchen

Vegan cooking with an edge. Free recipes, including categories for low fat, no refined sugar, and wheat free.

www.theppk.com/recipes

Slow Cookers

A Year of Slow Cooking

In 2008, Stephanie O'Dea made a resolution to use her slow cooker every day for a year; this blog chronicled her journey. The *New York Times* bestselling author continues to release new recipes on her blog.

http://crockpot365.blogspot.com

Standard U.S./Metric Measurement Conversions

VOLUME CONVERSIONS

U.S. Volume Measure	Metric Equivalent
⅛ teaspoon	0.5 milliliters
¼ teaspoon	1 milliliters
½ teaspoon	2 milliliters
1 teaspoon	5 milliliters
½ tablespoon	7 milliliters
1 tablespoon (3 teaspoons)	15 milliliters
2 tablespoons (1 fluid ounce)	30 milliliters
¼ cup (4 tablespoons)	60 milliliters
⅓ cup	90 milliliters
½ cup (4 fluid ounces)	125 milliliters
⅔ cup	160 milliliters
¾ cup (6 fluid ounces)	180 milliliters
1 cup (16 tablespoons)	250 milliliters
1 pint (2 cups)	500 milliliters
1 quart (4 cups)	1 liter (about)

WEIGHT CONVERSIONS

U.S. Weight Measure	Metric Equivalent
½ ounce	15 grams
1 ounce	30 grams
2 ounces	60 grams
3 ounces	85 grams
¼ pound (4 ounces)	115 grams
½ pound (8 ounces)	225 grams
¾ pound (12 ounces)	340 grams
1 pound (16 ounces)	454 grams

OVEN TEMPERATURE CONVERSIONS

Degrees Fahrenheit	Degrees Celsius
200 degrees F	95 degrees C
250 degrees F	120 degrees C
275 degrees F	135 degrees C
300 degrees F	150 degrees C
325 degrees F	160 degrees C
350 degrees F	180 degrees C
375 degrees F	190 degrees C
400 degrees F	205 degrees C
425 degrees F	220 degrees C
450 degrees F	230 degrees C

BAKING PAN SIZES

American	Metric
8 × 1½ inch round baking pan	20 × 4 cm cake tin
9 × 1½ inch round baking pan	23 × 3.5 cm cake tin
11 × 7 × 1½ inch baking pan	28 × 18 × 4 cm baking tin
13 × 9 × 2 inch baking pan	30 × 20 × 5 cm baking tin
2-quart rectangular baking dish	30 × 20 × 3 cm baking tin
15 × 10 × 2 inch baking pan	30 × 25 × 2 cm baking tin (Swiss roll tin)
9-inch pie plate	22 × 4 or 23 × 4 cm pie plate
7- or 8-inch springform pan	18- or 20-cm springform or loose-bottom cake tin
9 × 5 × 3 inch loaf pan	23 × 13 × 7 cm or 2 lb narrow loaf or pate tin
1½-quart casserole	1.5-liter casserole
2-quart casserole	2-liter casserole

Index

We Have

EVERYTHING® on Anything!

With more than 19 million copies sold, **the Everything® series** has become one of America's favorite resources for solving problems, learning new skills, and organizing lives. Our brand is not only recognizable—it's also welcomed.

The series is a hand-in-hand partner for people who are ready to tackle new subjects—like you!

For more information on the Everything® series, please visit *www.adamsmedia.com*

The Everything® list spans a wide range of subjects, with more than 500 titles covering 25 different categories:

Business	History	Reference
Careers	Home Improvement	Religion
Children's Storybooks	Everything Kids	Self-Help
Computers	Languages	Sports & Fitness
Cooking	Music	Travel
Crafts and Hobbies	New Age	Wedding
Education/Schools	Parenting	Writing
Games and Puzzles	Personal Finance	
Health	Pets	